This Book is Presented To

_____

By

_____

The Backstory of Where Jesus Was Born

Ron A. Bishop

ISBN (print): 978-0-9973515-4-5

ISBN (kindle): 978-0-9973515-5-2

Cover Painting: Gwynne Rohrs

Prepared for Publication by www.palmtreeproductions.com

To Contact the Author:

WWW.SHEPHERDSHAPERS.COM

"No other day on the calendar catches the imagination of young and old alike as does Christmas. It's a high and holy day—a day when the veil is drawn back and we get a fresh view of eternity. Such a vision of truth should be spread near and far."

—Billy Graham

CONTENTS

Acknowledgements

I would like to acknowledge a number of people who were instrumental in supporting me in the writing of this book. Special thanks go to my entire family for always being there for me and for making me proud.

- I want to thank my wife, Christina Reed Bishop, for her continual help, support, and patience with me through fifty wonderful years of marriage, countless ministry and missionary ventures, and all my book projects, including this one.

- I want to thank my son, Cameron, and his wife, Letha, and their children, Lauren, Trent, and Cole, and Cole's wife, Julia, for their constant love and support.

- I want to thank my daughter, Dory, and her husband, Joseph Rohrs, for their love, and support, as well as their work on the cover of the book, in spite of their busy schedules. I also want to thank their children, Gwynne, Cyrus, and Cora Rohrs for their love and support. And a special thanks to Gwynne for creating the beautiful painting on the book cover.

- I would like to thank my friend, Diana Baker, (author, editor, and pastor) for her labor of love in editing this book.

- I would especially like to thank Wendy Walters and Palm Tree Productions for making my words look great on the page, for their professionalism, and for publishing this book in a timely manner.

PROLOGUE

THE BACKSTORY OF WHERE JESUS WAS BORN is a real life story. It's so gripping, it's better than a drama or anything theater could produce. It's the introduction of "Redemption" set in a small Middle Eastern town we now know as Bethlehem.

The names listed below are people God appointed to send a strong message to mankind. Not only did He set the stage, but He breathed life into "real-life" people so powerfully that the story can only be described as "World Class" or "A Listed."

This is an old story, but as you read, you may find the events coming alive to you in a way you never understood before, almost as if its brilliant secrets eluded you up until now. You may even find yourself sitting on the edge of your seat when you picture these "nail biting events" as they unfold before your eyes.

The following people all lived, worked or walked on the site, which was the "place where Jesus was born."

Just a few of the people who lived, walked or worked on this land were: Salmon and Rahab, Boaz and Ruth, Obed, Jesse and David, Samuel (the prophet), Chimham, Jeremiah (the Prophet), Mary and Joseph, lots of shepherds, the Magi, and even some of Herod's army.

Some have said, "The **people** made this place famous." I say, "The **Birth of Jesus** made this place famous."

Chapter 1

THE BIRTH OF JOHN THE BAPTIST

The Birth of Jesus is so significant that it serves as the watershed for all of history.[1] From the days of Jesus, we look back at history and then afterward to all that has followed.

All through history, in every culture of the world, in advance of Royalty coming through a village or town, someone is sent ahead to announce the event so all of his/her loyal subjects may prepare themselves for a proper and appropriate response. The messenger may blow a trumpet to announce the event. In response, the people may clap their hands, bow their knees, line the streets as they would for a parade, or sing songs of love and respect similar to "God save the Queen." Whatever the case, wherever the culture, royal people do not just arrive; they are met with an attitude of gratitude if not obeisance.

THE STORY OF THE BIRTH OF THE MESSIAH CANNOT BEGIN TO BE TOLD ... UNTIL THE FORERUNNER HAS BEEN BORN.

This announcement as the "forerunner" was the assignment for John the Baptist, and he did it well. In that case, the coming of heaven's Messiah was to be announced, applauded, and by all means, gifts were to be given by the respectful. All that would come in time, but the coming of the Messiah had to be properly announced.

Finally, the very generation to see the Messiah and to be his contemporaries had been born, and so it was time for the Royalty of Heaven to come to mankind.

JOHN THE BAPTIST'S MESSAGE STYLE WAS MUCH LIKE A TRUMPET SOUND TO THE LISTENING EARS.

In preparing for that moment, let us go to Jerusalem and to the Temple itself for "the announcement of the forerunner," and to his father, a Levitical priest by the name of Zacharias.

The prophets had much to say as they spoke of how the Messiah would come and bring salvation. The timetable was set into motion when a Jewish priest named Zacharias[2] was appointed through the customary casting of lots to burn incense in the Temple. This duty was generally known as a "once in a lifetime" opportunity for a priest.

Gabriel Visited Zacharias in the Temple

More than 700 years before the advent of Jesus, the prophet Isaiah had observed the events and predicted them accurately. He could see through the prophetic eyes of God that before Jesus arrived, a forerunner would come to southern Judea, who would be described as a "voice crying in the wilderness."[3] That man would be John the Baptist who came declaring,

I am the voice of one crying in the wilderness:
Make straight the way of the Lord,
as the prophet Isaiah said.[4]

The plan of God and the calendar of heaven had been set on a schedule from ancient times. The prophets had prophesied, and the seers[5] and watchers[6] were waiting with bated breath for everything to align with the very heartbeat of God. The local hardships and political challenges of that day denied that the Messiah would make his grand entrance then. Still, the precise timing of events was already being orchestrated from the throne room of heaven.

JOHN WAS LIKE A TRUMPET, THE VOICE OF ONE MAN PROCLAIMING THAT MEN EVERYWHERE MUST PREPARE THEIR HEARTS BECAUSE, "THE KING IS COMING!"

The divine clock began ticking at exactly the time when Zacharias, a Levitical priest, entered the Holy Place in the Temple in Jerusalem to offer incense. The stopwatch was then activated, and the plan of God for the Redemption of mankind shifted into action as the Archangel Gabriel[7] left heaven for earth. Within six months, Gabriel would also visit Mary, a full 65 miles (105 km) away.

Zacharias was assuming his priestly role of burning incense in the Temple that week according to the ordered schedule. He had been selected by the casting of lots, but certainly, that was no accident or mistake. The landing of the lot upon Zacharias was by the plan of God. That would be Zacharias' first and only time to serve in the Holy Place.[8]

On that particular day, a great crowd of people had gathered to pray for Zacharias as he entered the Holy Place. As a matter of course, he stepped into his role and began burning the incense. Suddenly, he was thrown into consternation when he observed through the dim lights of the chamber an angel of the Lord standing off to the right of the incense altar. He was terrified and became visibly "shaken and overwhelmed"[9] with fear at the sight.

TAKE TIME TO READ THE ENTIRE STORY ABOUT JOHN'S BIRTH BY READING LUKE 1:5-2:20.

The angel Gabriel said, 'Do not be afraid, Zacharias, for God has heard your prayer. Your wife, Elizabeth, will give you a son and you are to name him John. You will have great joy and happiness will come to you. As a result of John's birth and what he will do in life, many will rejoice and the Lord will use Him to turn many Israelites to the Lord. He must never drink wine nor strong drink; and he shall be filled with the Holy Ghost, even from his mother's womb. John will be set apart to challenge Israel, and he shall be great in the eyes of the Lord, for he will turn many Israelites to the Lord their God.

The spirit and power of Elijah will come upon him. He will help to prepare the people for the coming of the Messiah. He will turn the hearts of the fathers to their children, and he will cause those who are rebellious to accept the wisdom of the godly.'

Zacharias was so stunned by those words, and by being visited in the Holy Place by Gabriel himself that he said, "How is this possible? How am I to believe all that you have said to me? After all,

I am an old man, and my wife, Elizabeth, is well past the years of childbearing. I cannot wrap my thoughts around what you're saying to me. How can I be sure this will happen?"[10]

Unfortunately, Zacharias[11] was absolutely blindsided by Gabriel's visit because he was totally unaware of the strategic role he would play in heaven's historic business. He had not seen the divine favor of Gabriel's visit with a heart of hope, expectation, and wonder but had seen it with surprise and the fear that he might not have what it took to fulfill God's plan. He likely knew God was able to perform the work, but he was doubtful that he would be able to do his part. In short, Zacharias was over-analyzing his own role.

It was at that point, the angel responded with authority and total clarity, saying, "I am Gabriel! I stand in the very presence of God! It was he who sent me to bring you this good news, but since you didn't believe what I said, you will be silent and unable to speak until the child is born. For my words will certainly be fulfilled at the proper time."

EVERY TIME GABRIEL SHOWS UP IN THE BIBLE, HE MAKES MENTION OF JESUS. GABRIEL'S MESSAGES ALWAYS POINT TO THE COMING MESSIAH.

Many people were gathered outside the Temple, praying and waiting for Zacharias to complete his work inside. They were excited because the burning of incense was only done once a year. Eventually it became evident that Zacharias was taking longer than usual to perform his duties, and the people wondered why. When he finally exited the Holy Place, noticeably moved and unable to speak, many agreed he must have seen a vision.

After Zacharias finished his week of service in the Temple, he returned home. During the following nine months, it became totally clear to him that every word spoken by the angel would be fulfilled. He had no doubt in his heart.

Elizabeth Deals with Being Pregnant in Her Old Age

It had not taken long after Zacharias' return home from the Temple for Elizabeth to conceive a child. As shocked as Zacharias had been at hearing the words of Gabriel, it must have been like a twilight zone moment for Elizabeth to discover that changes were taking place in her body that were clear signs of pregnancy. Upon becoming fully aware of what was happening to her, she chose to deal with it by going into seclusion for five months. Some of her challenges were having friends, family members, and neighbors gawk at her because of the anomaly of her being pregnant at her age.

However, from her joyful perspective, she exclaimed, "How kind the Lord is, for He has taken away my disgrace of having no children."[12]

Joseph and Mary Are Betrothed to Be Married

According to the Hebrew custom, Joseph, a direct descendant of King David, had approached the parents of a young virgin named Mary, also a direct descendant of David, while she was still in her teens and had agreed to pay to her father the bride price.[13] The couple had then become betrothed or engaged. This contractual agreement was binding upon Joseph, Mary, and her parents for a year.[14]

Joseph would have committed to prepare a home for himself and Mary, so that at any point, the other arrangements could be made. Mary's part of the agreement would have sounded something like this: "You are betrothed to Joseph.[15] That means that you are his wife in everything except that which pertains to family."[16]

Gabriel's Announcement to the Young Virgin Mary

Elizabeth progressed into her pregnancy by completing her ritual time of seclusion. She had been back in her home for about a month when Gabriel was dispatched by God to the city of Nazareth in Galilee.

FAITH THRIVES OUTSIDE THE REALM OF THE NATURAL MIND.

At that time, Mary, being young, perhaps felt awkward and wondered why she should be married at a time when she still saw herself as a child. She was shy, timid, and quite hesitant at all that this new relationship would bring into her life. Not knowing just how she felt about it, she had pulled aside to figure things out.

During one of those moments, Mary saw a strange figure near her. She was drawn to the angelic presence and not as bothered by it as Zacharias had been. Instead, she was curious and drew closer so she could see him better.

THE MIND CANNOT SPEAK THE LANGUAGE OF THE SPIRIT.

WHEN YOUR MIND DOESN'T HAVE A CLUE, PUT YOUR HEART OUT FRONT AND TALK TO THE LORD.

She realized the presence was not intrusive or invasive but was gentle, for the angel, exuding the very spirit of God said, "Rejoice, highly favored one, the Lord is with you: blessed are you among women."[17]

As strange as it seemed, Mary realized that Gabriel's words were directed at her. To a young virgin girl, this greeting perhaps seemed too formal and holy and was not the style of greeting she would have expected. She realized this was clearly not an ordinary man, and yet, there was a calming effect within her as she heard him speak. As surreal as it felt, she knew there was some strange truth to his words when he declared,

> 'Do not be afraid, Mary, for you have found favor with God. Listen carefully, for you will conceive, in your womb, and give birth to a son, and you shall name Him Jesus. He will be very great and will be called the Son of the Most High. The Lord God will give him the throne of his ancestor David. And he will reign over Israel forever; his Kingdom will never end!'

> Mary asked, 'But how can this be, since I do not know a man?' And the angel answered and said to her, 'The Holy Spirit will come upon you, and the power of the Highest will overshadow you; therefore, also, that Holy One who is to be born will be called the Son of God. Now indeed, Elizabeth your "cousin" has also conceived a son in her old age; and this is now the sixth month for her who was called barren. For with God nothing will be impossible.' [18]

> Mary said, 'Behold the maidservant of the Lord! Let it be to me according to your word.' Then the angel departed from her.

Elizabeth Hosted Mary for Three Months

The visit by Gabriel made a huge impression on young Mary. She found it comforting to realize that her pregnancy and the pregnancy of her cousin Elizabeth were both miraculous and somehow connected to a divine plan. While she was young, and Elizabeth was past the normal childbearing age, God was bringing miraculous blessings with a wonderful outcome upon them both. She felt compelled to investigate by visiting her cousin.

Mary's parents most likely saw her request as untimely and inconvenient, especially in light of the safety issues that made it dangerous for a young girl to travel alone. However, they helped her arrange to travel with friends on the journey. It's unlikely that they knew anything at that time of the angelic visit or the unexpected pregnancy of their daughter.

Mary's emotions must have been overwhelming since they prompted and pressed her to take an adventurous journey to discover the facts. Adulthood had come to her life quickly, and she now faced the world from a different perspective. She sensed the very presence of God in a different way than ever before.

Mary would later discover that she was not the only one who had received a visit from the Angel Gabriel. He had also visited Zacharias, Elizabeth's husband. This confirmation would give Mary the faith and stamina to press onward, even in the midst of criticism and doubt. In Mary's heart of hearts, she would take courage in the credibility of her own miracle when she heard the story, which gave credence to Elizabeth's miracle.

All Mary could think of as she prepared for her journey was that there was a miracle in both her pregnancy and Elizabeth's. She felt compelled to find out how and why they were the recipients of such miracles.

The journey to the Judean hill country, which is thought to be traditionally the village of Ein Karem or Beth Hakerem[19] just outside the city of Jerusalem, took several days of travel. When Mary arrived at her destination, she entered Elizabeth's home unannounced. When Elizabeth heard Mary's greeting, her baby moved within her.

The Holy Spirit came upon Elizabeth.
Then in a loud voice she said to Mary:
'God has blessed you more than any other woman!
He has also blessed the child you will have.
Why should the mother of my Lord come to me?
As soon as I heard your greeting,
my baby became happy and moved within me.
The Lord has blessed you because you believed
that he will keep his promise.' [20]

Notice the contrast between Zacharias' skepticism and doubt when Gabriel appeared to him and Mary's immediate belief in the angel and his words to her. Because of Zacharias' doubt, he was stricken mute until his baby's birth, whereas Mary was commended by God through her cousin Elizabeth for her simple faith and trust in Him. (Too often we, like Zacharias, resist trusting God because our human hearts put up barriers, and we fear we will appear gullible and naïve.)

Mary's visit with Elizabeth lasted about three months.[21] During that time, Mary enjoyed the companionship of her older cousin, who likely served as a much-needed mentor to diminish her fears and balance her perspectives, in light of the fact that they were both on divine assignments.

Baby John Would Become the Forerunner of the Christ

These divine assignments would be seen throughout history as world-changing.[22] Baby John would become the forerunner of the Christ and be known as "John the Baptist." His primary message was, "Repent for the Messiah is coming."

The Gospel of Mark actually starts off with these words:

The good news of Jesus Christ—the Message!—begins here, following to the letter the scroll of the prophet Isaiah. Watch closely: I'm sending my preacher ahead of you; He'll make the road smooth for you. Thunder in the desert! Prepare for God's arrival! Make the road smooth and straight!' [23]

The child who would be born to Mary and Joseph was the long-awaited Messiah, who would come to redeem the sins of the world.

THE PREACHING OF JOHN
THE BAPTIST CREATED
MORE EXCITEMENT THAN
ANY MESSAGE EVER SPOKEN
IN ALL OF HISTORY!
THE MASSES KEPT COMING
TO LISTEN AND TO REPENT.

Chapter 2

THE BIRTH OF JESUS, THE CHRIST

Mary Returned to Nazareth and a Bewildered Joseph

There was a serious awkwardness when Mary arrived back at her home in Nazareth. She was three months pregnant, and it was obvious. It created a stir in her family, community, and especially with Joseph, her betrothed husband. Doubts and strong concerns were evident because this was the "first time" in history a virgin had ever conceived a child, and it would be the last.

NO WONDER THEY WERE SURPRISED! THIS WAS THE "FIRST TIME" IN ALL OF HISTORY IT HAD EVER OCCURRED, AND IT WOULD NEVER HAPPEN AGAIN.

In the Old Testament, miracles had taken place. Men had been raised from the dead[1], leprosy had been healed[2], etc., but never had a conception taken place without sexual intercourse between a man and a woman. There was even talk about stoning Mary.

An Angel from the Lord Visited Joseph in a Dream

God knew society was full of doubt and would be unable to understand what was really going on with the birth of Jesus Christ, so he sent an angel to visit Joseph in a dream. Mary's husband Joseph was a righteous man. Because he didn't want to humiliate Mary, he decided to call off their engagement quietly.

As he was thinking about this, an angel from the Lord appeared to him in a dream and said,

> *"Joseph son of David,*
> *don't be afraid to take Mary as your wife,*
> *because the child she carries*
> *was conceived by the Holy Spirit.*
> *She will give birth to a son, and you will call him Jesus,*
> *because he will save his people from their sins."*
> *Now all of this took place so that what the Lord had*
> *spoken through the prophet would be fulfilled:*
> *"Look! A virgin will become pregnant and give birth to a*
> *son, and they will call him, Emmanuel."*
> *(Emmanuel means "God with us.")*

When Joseph woke up, he obeyed God's command through the angel and took Mary as his wife. But he didn't have sexual relations with her until she gave birth to a son. Joseph called the son Jesus.[3]"

Their Journey Was to Bethlehem. Why Bethlehem?

Just weeks before Mary should be planning for the birth of Jesus, word came in an edict announced by Herod's soldiers that Caesar Augustus required everyone to be registered in their birth country.

This census first took place while Quirinius was governing Syria. So, all went to be registered, everyone to his own city. Joseph also went up from Galilee, out of the city of Nazareth, into Judea, to the city of David, which is called Bethlehem, because he was of the house and lineage of David, to be registered with Mary, his betrothed wife, who was with child.

So it was, that while they were there, the days were completed for her to be delivered. And she brought forth her firstborn Son, and wrapped Him in swaddling cloths[4] and laid Him in a manger, because there was no room for them in the inn.[5]

Joseph told Mary's parents he needed to take his wife with him to the city of Bethlehem, his ancestral home. Her parents were concerned since she was so far along in her pregnancy, but they agreed that there were no choices because of Herod's requirements.

The trip would span nearly 100 miles and would take perhaps as long as 7-10 days because of Mary's condition and the route they had to travel.[6] Traveling conditions were uncomfortable and tiring, since they had no cart or wagon in which to ride and carry supplies and only one donkey for Mary to ride. And there was little food available other than flat bread and a few other supplies they purchased at villages along the way.

Finally they could see the city of Bethlehem in the distance. When they arrived, they knew Mary's time to deliver her baby was imminent, so they immediately looked for a place to stay. But there were no vacancies—no room in the Inn for her to rest.[7]

It seemed that the host of the Inn was kind and offered his only option, a grotto[8] behind the Inn which served as his stable. The challenge was that their sleeping arrangements required them to cohabit the space with sheep, chickens, and other farm animals. As inconvenient as it appeared, they were glad for a place to stay.

Almost immediately, Mary's contractions began. When the child was born, they laid him in a manger filled with straw. Mary gathered the pieces of cloth she had brought to swaddle the newborn in so he would feel safe and secure, warm, and at peace.

Glory in the Highest

Shepherds were all around Bethlehem in the fields that night. It was a sleepy, quiet night, and they were lingering between drowsiness and keeping a watchful eye on their sheep. Suddenly their senses were awakened, and they became aware of a host of angels gathering above them in the open skies.

This is what one writer recorded in an ancient manuscript regarding the events of that evening: "While attending to their sheep, the night being cold and chilly, some of the shepherds had made fires to warm themselves, and some of them had laid down and were asleep. They were awakened by those who were keeping watch who asked, 'What does all this mean? Behold, how light it is.' When they were aroused it was light as day. But they knew it was not daylight, for it was only the third watch."[9]

They watched in awe as the skyline became alive with music and an angel of the Lord stood before them and declared,

THE SHEPHERDS WERE WATCHING THEIR SHEEP ON THE HILLS JUST OUTSIDE OF BETHLEHEM AND WITHIN DIRECT VISUAL SIGHT OF BOAZ'S FIELD WHERE RUTH HAD GLEANED (1300 BC), AND WHERE DAVID HAD WATCHED HIS SHEEP (1000 BC). IT WAS A SMALL AREA WITHIN SIGHT OF CHIMHAM'S INN, BEHIND WHICH WAS THE GROTTO IN WHICH JESUS WAS BORN.

'Do not be afraid, for behold, I bring you good tidings of Great joy which will be to all people. For there is born to you this day in the city of David a Savior, who is Christ the Lord. And this will be the sign to you: You will find a Babe wrapped in swaddling clothes, lying in a manger.'

And suddenly there was with the angel a multitude of the heavenly host praising God and saying, 'Glory to God in the highest, and on earth peace, goodwill toward men!'

When the angels had gone away from them into heaven, the shepherds said to one another, "Let us now go to Bethlehem and see this thing that has come to pass, which the Lord has made known to us."[10]

It was only a short while before the procession of shepherds arrived at the grotto. They gathered near the manger with reverent awe and payed homage, celebrating the savior who had come to bring them salvation. They had seen the focused light of the star and could not resist following it. It was an amazing and affirming moment for Mary and Joseph.

The Wise Men from the East Came to See Jesus

It states in Matthew 2:1, "Now after Jesus was born in Bethlehem of Judea in the days of Herod, behold wise men from the East came to Jerusalem."[11]

THE WISE MEN KNEW THERE WAS ANOTHER DIMENSION WHICH ALLOWED FOR HEAVEN'S INPUT … THE VOICE OF THE PROPHETIC. IN OTHER WORDS: LISTEN UP! "GOD SPEAKS TO US THROUGH PROPHETS."

The Magi, or as they're often called, "the wise men," were most likely from Persia or even as far east as Afghanistan. They were astronomers[12] who spent their lives studying the placement of the stars as well as historical documents, manuscripts, and prophetic writings. They apparently had some knowledge of Israel and the Hebrew tradition. If their home country had been too great a distance away from Israel, they would not have had an awareness of the culture of such a nation. That is another reason to consider Persia (modern day Iran) as their home.

One thing is certain: "Christian Theological tradition has always stressed that Gentiles, as well as Jews, came to worship Jesus."[13]

32

The story in Matthew is that these Magi came to Jerusalem, Israel's capital, and found themselves face to face with King Herod I, king of Judea. They asked Herod:

'Where is He who has been born King of the Jews? For we have seen His star in the East and have come to worship Him.'

When Herod the king heard this, he was troubled, and all Jerusalem with him. And when he had gathered all the chief priests and scribes of the people together, he inquired of them where the Christ was to be born.

So they said to him, 'In Bethlehem of Judea, for thus it is written by the prophet:

But you, Bethlehem, in the land of Judah,

Are not the least among the rulers of Judah;

For out of you shall come a Ruler

Who will shepherd My people Israel.'

Then Herod, when he had secretly called the wise men, determined from them what time the star appeared. And he sent them to Bethlehem and said, 'Go and search carefully for the young Child, and when you have found Him, bring back word to me, that I may come and worship Him also.'

The Wise Men and the First Baby Shower

When the Magi, or wise men, had finished their visit with King Herod, "they departed; and behold, the Star[14] which they had seen in the East went before them, till it came and stood over the entire place where the young Child was."[15]

Clearly the child was in Bethlehem, as the entire story of the Magi and Herod centered on the prophecies of the Messiah being born in Bethlehem. Since Mary and Joseph are only known to have been in Bethlehem at the time of Jesus' birth, and perhaps shortly afterwards, it is not difficult to know Jesus' age during this visit.[16]

The place where Jesus was born was a historical site. Its history extended all the way back through the days of Jeremiah,[17] to the days when David lived there, and farther back to the time of the division of the land. That piece of land had been given by Joshua to Salmon (and his wife Rahab). It was the home of Boaz and contained the field where Ruth had gleaned behind the reapers. It was also David's inheritance which he had given to Chimham, the son of Barzillai. David had promised Barzillai, "If you send Chimham, in your stead, I will bestow upon him all sorts of good things."[18]

KEEP IN MIND THAT THE INN KEEPER MUST HAVE NOTICED ALL THE ACTIVITY AROUND THE GROTTO ON HIS LAND WITH HIS ANIMALS. HE MAY HAVE INVITED JOSEPH AND MARY INTO THE INN FOR THE NEXT NIGHT IF A ROOM WAS AVAILABLE.

Jesus was born in the grotto behind the Inn.[19] It's likely that after the initial night of Jesus' birth, hospitality was extended and an invitation was made for the young family to find more comfort in the Inn.[20] The Inn was not designed like a hotel room. It was an arrangement of basic rooms around an open-air courtyard. All Middle Eastern homes were simple rooms around a central courtyard. The cooking area was outside around a fire pit of some type.[21]

One thousand years had passed from the time King David had lived in Bethlehem. There had been many born into his family line, not to mention all the other families which had spawned from Bethlehem. There was no local infrastructure to support the many weary travelers who had made the journey to the city. They arrived in the town and stayed where they could: some in the Inn or in homes, and some even camping out with the shepherds on the hillsides.

It has always been the culture of the Middle East to be "friendly and hospitable to strangers." It appears quite likely that the dwelling place or Inn of Chimham's, which had been birthed in his heart so long ago, had continued operating as a friendly place to come when traveling through Bethlehem. It was not a tavern but certainly a home away from home, a place to refresh for the continuing journey.

THE REASON THERE WAS NO ROOM IN THE INN WAS BECAUSE OF THE SPIKE IN TRAVELERS WHO HAD TRAVELED TO BETHLEHEM IN COMPLIANCE WITH THE ORDER OF CAESAR AUGUSTUS TO "REGISTER IN THEIR OWN HOME CITY."

After the night Jesus was born in the place behind the Inn, on the same property where David had spent his childhood, it's likely that many had completed their task of registering their kinship to satisfy Rome's edict and had begun their return journey to their homes.

A question that's often asked is: "How long did the star of Bethlehem direct its focus on the property of Chimham before it dissipated? Did it last a single night, or even as some have suggested, as long as up to seventy days, as unlikely as that may be?"[22] We don't know how long the Star was shining, but it certainly served the Magi well in leading them to Bethlehem and the place of Jesus' birth.

> *When the Magi saw the star, they rejoiced with exceedingly great joy. And when they had come into the house, they saw the young Child with Mary His mother, and fell down and worshipped Him. And when they had opened their treasures, they presented gifts to Him: 'gold, frankincense, and myrrh*[23]

It would have been expected that Jesus was taken to the local synagogue on the eighth day to be circumcised and given the name Jesus. Although we don't know the exact day after Jesus' birth the Magi came to see the newborn "King of the Jews," it was certainly while the family remained in Bethlehem.

When the Magi arrived, they knelt before the child and his family, giving full acknowledgement of who this infant was. They then portrayed the sincerity of their purpose by giving the family the valuable gifts they had brought.

The Magi had put lots of thought into selecting appropriate gifts to give to a "King." Although we don't know how many Magi came, it is traditionally thought to be three, largely because three gifts were given. We do know that they were recognized as kings in their own home countries, so they were giving gifts appropriate to their status in life. We recognize that they chose their gifts carefully and are awed today at the sophistication of their choices.[24]

These Magi did not stay long. It is likely they only spent a night or two to rest before their journey home. During their last night in Bethlehem, the Lord gave them a dream instructing them to return home by a different route and to not report back to Herod.

After the Magi departed, Joseph also received a dream from the Lord.

An angel of the Lord appeared to Joseph in a dream,
saying, 'Arise, take the young Child and His mother, flee
to Egypt, and stay there until I bring you word;
for Herod will seek the young Child to destroy Him.'
When he arose, he took the young Child and His mother
by night and departed for Egypt.[25]

We don't know much about their journey to Egypt, but we can verify that the nearest point in Egypt to which they could have gone[26] that would have gotten them across a border and away from Herod's jurisdiction was as short as 65 kilometers (40 miles).[27]

It's reasonable to expect that for the sake of convenience they chose to travel "The King's Highway,"[28] which lay beside the Mediterranean Sea. After all, they only had one donkey to carry Mary and Jesus, and Joseph had to walk the entire distance.

The Massacre of Innocent Children

Herod was paranoid and obviously aware of the civil unrest and undercurrents against his rule. He was determined to deal swiftly with any talk of insurrection. He did not realize that his own days were in short supply.[29]

When Herod realized the Magi had not returned to him as he had asked, he panicked and flew into a rage. To make sure the newborn child was slain so he wouldn't pose a threat to his rule, he ordered his soldiers to travel to Bethlehem and slay every male child two years old or younger. Unconcerned about how many children would die, he took a broad swath of ages to make sure the young king would be killed.

Over the years, Herod had already ordered the assassination of many whom he considered to be a threat to his reign, including his father-in-law, several of his ten wives, and two of his sons.[30]

Jesus Was Safe from Herod

When Herod died, an angel of the Lord appeared in a dream to Joseph[31] in Egypt. 'Get up!' the angel said. 'Take the child and his mother back to the land of Israel because those who were trying to kill the child are dead.' So Joseph got up from his sleep and returned to the land of Israel with Jesus and his mother.

The Return to Nazareth

The journey from Egypt to Nazareth was long and hard. As they traveled by foot, the road passed close enough to Jerusalem for Mary to be able to go to the Temple and fulfill the requirements of her purification ceremony.[32] Everything was falling into place. Joseph, Mary, and Jesus had been kept safe from Herod, and now Mary would be able to meet the requirements of the Law of Moses.

Simeon Recognizes the Messiah

While in Jerusalem, Mary and Joseph were able to present Jesus to the Lord in the Temple. As they approached the Rabbi to make the customary dedication of their firstborn son, an older man hurried to them. He was a righteous and devout man named Simeon who was seen daily in the temple, often speaking out in a prophetic way about how the Lord would soon send a deliverer, the Messiah, who would save his people.

Simeon, reached out and reverently asked the young parents if he could hold the child. As he reached for the infant, he began to quiver and rejoice and praise the God of heaven for giving him that moment to see the Lord's Messiah with his own eyes. He exclaimed that the Holy Spirit had revealed that he would not see death until "first I would see the Lord's Messiah."

Simeon lifted up his voice in prayer and prayed,

> *Lord, I am your servant, and now I can die in peace,*
> *because you have kept your promise to me.*
> *With my own eyes I have seen what you have done*
> *to save your people, and foreign nations will also see this.*
> *Your mighty power is a light for all nations,*
> *and it will bring honor to your people Israel.*

Joseph and Mary were surprised at Simeon's words. Simeon blessed them then prophesied these words to Mary,

> *This child of yours will cause many people*
> *in Israel to fall and others to stand.*
> *The child will be like a warning sign.*
> *Many people will reject him, and you,*
> *Mary, will suffer as though you had been*
> *stabbed by a dagger.*
> *But all this will show what people are really thinking.*[33]

A Prophetess Named Anna Came to See Jesus

On the same day in the Temple, there was a lady named Anna, a Prophetess[34] who was known for her personal devotion to God. She had married in her youth, but after only seven years she was widowed. She had been a widow for nearly sixty years and had dedicated her entire adult life to the service of the Lord. She was known by many as a woman given to prayer and fasting. Now at the age of 84, she had dedicated her time solely to encouraging others.

While Simeon held Jesus in his arms, Anna came near to see him. She glorified God for sending the Messiah to redeem His people. It must have been an amazing and gratifying time for this young family to have so much attention given to Jesus that day in the Temple.

Mary then entered into her ceremony of purification and offered up a sacrifice of a pair of turtle doves or two young pigeons. Joseph and Mary had finally completed everything the Law of the Lord had commanded.[35] It was now time to leave Jerusalem.

The Family Returned to Nazareth

The couple was now faced with a crucial decision. It appears that they had been inclined to settle in Bethlehem of Judea. But Joseph had learned that the new ruler of Judea was Herod's son Archelaus, and he was afraid to go there. As he and Mary were considering where they would go, Joseph received a warning in a dream and felt he must take his family to the region of Galilee. This fulfilled what the prophets had said: "He will be called a Nazarene."[36] In the end, it proved to be a wise decision, especially since it was where they had lived during their earlier years.

> ## AUTHOR'S NOTE:
>
> DON'T BE CONFUSED BY DEPENDING ON HEROD'S COMMENTS TO SET THE TIME SCHEDULE FOR THESE EVENTS. AFTER ALL, THE STAR HAD LED THE MAGI FROM THEIR HOME COUNTRY TO BETHLEHEM BEFORE THEY MET HEROD. WE DON'T HAVE AN ABUNDANCE OF DETAILS TO HELP US DRAW A MORE SOLID CONCLUSION.
>
> THE STORY OF JESUS' BIRTH IS THE MAIN ISSUE TO FOCUS ON, NOT THE TIMING OF THE MAGI OR HEROD'S CONCLUSIONS ON TIMING. GOD'S TIMING HAS ALWAYS BEEN FLAWLESS, WHILE HEROD WAS AN IMPULSIVE, ANGRY, MURDERER ABOUT TO COME TO HIS OWN DEMISE.

It had been tempting to return to Bethlehem in Judea because they had found favor there. Still, Nazareth was where the Lord sent them, and their extended families would be a great encouragement and support to them.

"The Gospels do not tell us very much about Jesus' childhood; they focus instead on Jesus' public ministry, which only lasted around three years. Hundreds of years after Jesus lived on earth, some people made up stories about His childhood. But that's all they were … stories with no basis in fact."[37]

We do have one comment which was made by the leaders in the synagogue in Nazareth. Those men seemed to scoff at Jesus by saying, "'He's just a carpenter, the son of Mary and the brother of James, Joseph, Judas, and Simon. And his sisters live right here among us.' They were deeply offended and refused to believe in him."[38] It reminds us that Jesus knows what it is to work, and He has shared in the kind of life we experience."[39]

Twelve-year-old Jesus Amazed the Scholars

The childhood of Jesus was unique in a number of ways. He was able to grow up with his brothers, sisters,[40] cousins, grandparents, and other family members, but there were a number of experiences that challenged the adults in his life.

Joseph and Mary made a pilgrimage to Jerusalem every year at the time of the Feast of the Passover.

When Jesus was twelve years old, they went up to
Jerusalem according to the custom of the feast.
When they had finished the days, as they returned,
the Boy Jesus lingered behind in Jerusalem.

And Joseph and His mother did not know it;
but supposing Him to have been in the company,
they went a day's journey, and sought Him
among their relatives and acquaintances.
So when they did not find Him,
they returned to Jerusalem, seeking Him.

Now so it was that after three days they found Him
in the temple, sitting in the midst of the teachers,
both listening to them and asking them questions.

*And all who heard Him were astonished
at His understanding and answers.*

*So when they saw Him, they were amazed; and His
mother said to Him, 'Son, why have You done this to
us? Look, Your father and I have sought You anxiously.'*

*And He said to them, 'Why did you seek Me?
Did you not know that I must
be about My Father's business?'
But they did not understand the statement which He
spoke to them.*

*Then He went down with them and came to Nazareth,
and was subject to them, but His mother kept all these
things in her heart. And Jesus increased in wisdom and
stature, and in favor with God and men.*[41]

Chapter 3

THE BACKSTORY BEGINS

Joshua Ordered the Dividing of Canaan

The backstory began about 1400 years before the birth of Jesus Christ. The Israelites were standing facing Jericho, having just crossed on dry ground through the Jordan River.[1]

Since their Exodus from Egypt, they had already built a powerful history of miraculous and divine interventions. They had crossed on dry land through the Red Sea and had eaten "manna from heaven" for 40 years while wandering in the wilderness of Sinai. Canaan was now before them, and Jericho was in their sights.

Israel was united and encouraged because they had just heard the report of the two unnamed spies who said "all the people there shake with fear every time they think of us."[2] In giving their account to

Joshua, the spies spoke of the point of entry they'd chosen. It was the home of a prostitute named Rahab, who lived in an easily accessible house built on the Jericho city wall. Rahab had been hospitable to them, even though they were strangers, and it was fitting that she'd had a heart to help these men who posed such a threat to her city.

As strange as this story is, we see the hand of God at work. He had enabled and protected the spies while they were in Jericho to reconnoiter the region and the city. The spies were in great danger in Jericho, and Rahab was obviously in the position to give them aid when they needed it most. She opened her heart to the spies and spoke the following words to them concerning the fear she and her people had of the multitude of Hebrews:

> *I know that the LORD has given this land to your people.*
>
> *You frighten us.*
>
> *Everyone living in this country is afraid of you.*
>
> *We are afraid because we have heard about the ways that the LORD helped you.*
>
> *We heard that he dried up the Red Sea when you came out of Egypt.*
>
> *We also heard what you did to the two Amorite kings, Sihon and Og.*
>
> *We heard how you destroyed those kings living east of the Jordan River.*
>
> *When we heard this, we were very afraid.*
>
> *And now, not one of our men is brave enough to fight you, because the LORD your God rules the heavens above and the earth below!*

So now, I want you to make a promise to me.

I was kind to you and helped you.

So, promise me before the Lord that you will be kind to my family.

Please tell me that you will do this.

Tell me that you will allow my family to live—my father, mother, brothers, sisters, and all their families.

Promise me that you will save us from death.[3]

The stories of how God had miraculously delivered the Hebrew nation from slavery had preceded them and had caused Rahab's heart to reach out for favor from the two Israelite[4] spies and their God. Because of her acts of kindness in hiding the spies, they responded with commitments to guarantee her safety.

This is the simple chronology of how all the players entered this story from the longtime past:

- **Jacob** had a son named **Judah.**

- Judah had a son by Tamar[5] (his widowed daughter-in-law) whose name was **Perez.**

- Perez had a son named, **Hezron.**

- Hezron had a son named **Ram.**

- Ram fathered **Amminadab.**

- Amminadab fathered **Nahshon**, a leader of Judah.

- Nahshon had a son named **Salmon.**

- Salmon met and married **Rahab**, who had come from Jericho.[6]

Salmon joined with Joshua, as did all the men of Israel, and took the lands of Canaan which God had promised to Abraham 400 years earlier. The battles finally slowed down as the conquest began to accomplish its purpose. At that point, Joshua recognized that the families needed to settle into their new home.

> "NOT BECAUSE OF YOUR RIGHTEOUSNESS OR THE UPRIGHTNESS OF YOUR HEART ARE YOU GOING IN TO POSSESS THEIR LAND, BUT BECAUSE OF THE WICKEDNESS OF THESE NATIONS THE LORD YOUR GOD IS DRIVING THEM OUT FROM BEFORE YOU, AND THAT HE MAY CONFIRM THE WORD THAT THE LORD SWORE TO YOUR FATHERS, TO ABRAHAM, TO ISAAC, AND TO JACOB."
>
> DEUTERONOMY 9:5 NKJV

Joshua called all of the people together and through the casting of lots determined where every family should settle and where the various tribes would receive grants of land.[7] Those properties in Israel seldom changed hands, remaining in the hands of each family from generation to generation.

Salmon married Rahab, the harlot from Jericho, who had become part of the nation of Israel. Some scholars have speculated that Salmon may have been one of the two spies who had met her in her house on the city wall, but there is little evidence to back that opinion. We do know that Salmon received a grant of land from Joshua when all of Canaan was portioned off, divided, and given to the Israelites.[8] Salmon's parcel of land was just outside of the town of "Bethlehem Ephratah."[9] That land or inheritance belonging to Salmon became the host property and location of many historical events throughout Israel's history.

God blessed Salmon and Rahab with a son they named Boaz. Boaz inherited his father's land and became a man of influence and wealth.[10] His property contained the field where Ruth gleaned when she returned with Naomi from Moab. Boaz married Ruth, and they had a son named Obed. Obed lived on that land his entire life. He and his wife had a son named Jesse.

Jesse was blessed with seven sons. David was the youngest son of Jesse.[11] David was a shepherd and a musician and composed worship songs on the hillsides while he watched his sheep. Eventually he became known as "the sweet Psalmist of Israel." God sent Samuel to Bethlehem to anoint David as the new king who would one day replace Saul.

Later the property was inherited by Chimham, the son of Barzillai. He built an "Inn" there, and a caravansary[12] was eventually developed.

Several centuries later, Jeremiah the Prophet and several other captives stayed on the property while they were en route to Egypt.[13] A significant group of people were traveling with Johanan, as recorded in Jeremiah 41:11-17. Verse 17 says, *"And they departed and dwelt in the habitation of Chimham, which is near Bethlehem, as they went on their way to Egypt."* NKJV

Fourteen centuries later, that piece of property housed the grotto where Jesus was born.[14] As the New Testament opens, we find Joseph and Mary, who had traveled from Nazareth to Bethlehem, the city of David's birth, to be numbered in the census, ordered by Rome.[15] Since there was no room in the Inn, Mary and Joseph were taken to a place where there were two natural above ground grottos, only a few hundred meters apart. They were directed to one of those grottos where sheep and other livestock were kept. There Mary gave birth to Jesus and placed him in a manger.

Soon after Jesus' birth, the shepherds who had seen the angels and the heavenly choir of singers[16] visited the site to see him. Sometime after that, the Magi came bringing gifts for the "King of the Jews."[17] As you can see, there was a lot of activity on this family farm from the time of the entrance into Canaan when the land was divided until the time of Jesus' birth.

Chapter 4

DAVID AND A CIVIL WAR

AUTHOR'S NOTE:

THIS PART OF THE BACKSTORY IS NOT SO PLEASANT TO READ, BUT IN ORDER TO GRASP THE COMPLETE PICTURE, IT MUST BE TAKEN ON BOARD. I WILL SPARE YOU SOME OF THE MORE DISTASTEFUL PARTS, BUT I ALSO MUST NOT BE REMISS AND FAIL TO TELL THE BACKSTORY FULLY. THEN, PLEASE CONTINUE WITH ME AS WE READ ONWARD TO THE INSPIRATIONAL PARTS.

David's sin ten years prior to the civil war gave his enemies a cause that brought trouble to Israel. The backstory continues with dark clouds and a political storm brewing over the nation right in the middle of what is called "The Golden Age of Israel."[1]

David, the King, had sinned through an adulterous affair with the wife of Uriah, one of his Mighty Men.[2] David had then arranged for Uriah to be killed on the battlefield and had made sure it was hidden from the people.

The Holy Spirit revealed David's sin to the Prophet Nathan. Nathan went to the king's home on the morning of the birth of the child[3] conceived through David's sin, to confront David. The thunderous and throaty voice of the prophet echoed through the halls of the palace, as he forcefully declared his indictment, "Thou art the Man."[4]

Upon hearing the indictment, David immediately fell to his knees in repentance. He was just as quickly forgiven for his sin by the Lord God. The prophet was both judicial and merciful in nature. He was not halting in his indictment, nor was he reluctant in his announcement of the Lord's mercy.

It's clear that David first repented, and then the prophet Nathan declared that God had forgiven him. The "larger than life"[5] prophet, however, did not hesitate to inform the King that because of his selfish, inconsiderate violation of the laws of God, he and his descendants would suffer fallout. David would now "reap what he had sown."

Nathan's bold prophecy to David:

> *Now therefore, the sword shall never depart from your house, because you have despised Me, and have taken the wife of Uriah the Hittite to be your wife...*
> *Thus, saith the LORD.*

As the story continues, we see the prophecy being walked out in the rebellion of David's son, Prince Absalom.

Because of David's sin with Bathsheba and the death of her husband Uriah, it's apparent that David lost his grasp of judicial wisdom. That factor became evident in the way he addressed family conflicts in the following years. After Solomon became King, the family order was restored, but until then, David, the magnificent and intuitive leader, endured the results that came with the fallout from his own fleshly failures.

> BECAUSE OF HIS SIN, DAVID HAD LOST HIS GRASP OF PRECIOUS JUDICIAL WISDOM.

There was a storm brewing, and politically dark clouds were forming over the entire nation. All citizens were fearful of how this would affect their lives, their nation, and the Kingdom of Israel. The central player in the upheaval was Prince Absalom, who projected himself as a judge near the main gate of the capital city. For four years he gave flawed and divisive counsel to all who would listen. The people didn't seek his counsel. He approached them and prevailed upon them to listen to his side of the story. He aggressively sowed discord, and the people's hearts bent in his direction and away from King David. Absalom stole the hearts of all the men of Israel.[6]

Years later, Solomon penned the following words that were possibly inspired by that event:

> *There are six things the LORD hates—*
> *no, seven things he detests:*
> *haughty eyes, a lying tongue,*
> *hands that kill the innocent, a heart that plots evil,*
> *feet that race to do wrong, a false witness who pours out lies,*
> *a person who sows discord in a family.*[7]

It appears likely that because of what he had seen happen in his family, Solomon drew the conclusion that the worst of all the seven sins was number seven.

Absalom Declared a Coup d'état Against His Father, the King

One morning news spread everywhere declaring that Prince Absalom had departed the city with two hundred men running ahead of him to Hebron.[8] On the previous day, Absalom had sent spies throughout Israel telling the general populous of loyalists, "as soon as you hear the sound of the shofar[9], (trumpet) then you shall say, "Absalom reigns in Hebron!"[10] Someone loyal to King David immediately told David, "The hearts of the men of Israel are with Absalom."[11]

> "TO EVERY ACTION THERE IS ALWAYS AN EQUAL AND OPPOSITE, OR CONTRARY, REACTION."
>
> —ISAAC NEWTON

On the day after Absalom left for Hebron, news came that he had been hailed as the new king of the nation.[12] This proclamation would soon divide the reigning royal family.

Chaos filled the streets. Those who were loyal to Absalom seemed assured that things would go according to Absalom's plan. The greater majority, who were on David's side, had begun to pray for a good end to the hostilities.

Inside the palace, David wrestled with his own heart. He met with a trusted friend and ally, Zadok, the priest. A noted writer, Gene Edwards, sheds light on what their conversation may have been:

'What shall you do, David?

In your youth, you spoke no word against an unworthy king.

What shall you do now with an equally unworthy youth?'

David replied, 'These are the times I hate the most, Zadok.

Nonetheless, against all reason, I judge my own heart first and rule against its interests. I shall do what I did under Saul.

I shall leave the destiny of the Kingdom in God's hands alone.

It may be that He is finished with me.

Perhaps I have sinned too greatly and am no longer worthy to lead. Only God knows if that is true, and it seems He will not tell…

The throne is not mine. Not to have, not to take, not to protect, and not to keep. I shall leave the city.

The throne is the Lord's. So is the kingdom. I will not hinder God. No obstacle, no activity on my part lies in the space between God and His will. He has no hindrance to prevent Him from His will.

If I am not to be King, our God will find no difficulties in making Absalom to be Israel's king. Now it is possible. God shall be God.'

David turned and walked quietly out of the throne room, out of the palace, out of the city. He walked and he walked.[13]

It didn't take long for those near Jerusalem to see that the King, all the Royal family, and David's political leaders and friends had formed a large entourage and were leaving the city and heading northeast. Some rode horses and some had donkeys or wagons, but most of them were walking.

David Fled, Crossed Jordan, and Went to Mahanaim

As the King and his entourage trudged toward Gilgal and the western banks of the Jordan River, many things were happening in Jerusalem in the strategic planning sessions of Absalom and his counsellors. The decisions that were made there were secretly conveyed to David by his friends Hushai and the priests Zadok and Abiathar, who were posing as counsel and new friends to Absalom. The sons of these priests, Jonathan and Ahimaaz, quickly brought David news of the threats against him, warning David to not hesitate in the wilderness, but to pass over Jordan that night without delay.[14] The messengers said David's enemies would soon descend upon them should they fail to cross over the Jordan.

> DAVID THOUGHT: AM I STILL THE MAN WHOM GOD WOULD CHOOSE TO BE KING? WOULD GOD STILL PICK ME? PERHAPS THIS TIME HE WOULD CHOOSE ABSALOM OVER ME.

David and all those with him successfully passed over Jordan and "by daybreak, not even one was left who had not crossed the Jordan."[15] David had set out to make it all the way to Mahanaim. When morning came, they had all arrived at their destination, weary and hungry.

Chapter 5

BARZILLAI

A Friend When a Friend Was Desperately Needed

AUTHOR'S NOTE:

BARZILLAI WAS FROM THE HIGHLANDS OF ISRAEL'S EASTERN PLATEAU. WORLDWIDE AND THROUGHOUT HISTORY THE HIGHLANDS PRODUCED HARDY, HEALTHY, INDEPENDENT, FREETHINKING, HONEST, PEOPLE WITH GRASS-ROOTS INTEGRITY, THE BEDROCK OF LOYALTY, PATRIOTISM, AND STAMINA THAT EVERY ETH-NICITY NEEDS TO SURVIVE. THE FUEL FOR THAT CULTURE IS THAT IT IS REMOTE, RURAL, BACKWATER, AND OUTSIDE THE MAINSTREAM.

This part of the Backstory took place in Transjordan in eastern Israel. Three men from different cities and cultures with different life experiences and diverse family histories merged their lives when circumstances—a national civil war and political upheaval—became a reason to meet. This took place 3,000 years ago, around the year 1000 BC.

At first it wasn't apparent why they should join forces, but as their lives came under the influence of Barzillai,[1] the "peace broker," their hearts, viewpoints, and basic values all changed. He was the man who could and did make a difference on that day.

For a long time, Barzillai had been mentoring[2] an eclectic couple of men who only had him in common. Those students were Prince Shobi, son of Nahash from the Ammonite city of Rabbah, and Machir, son of Ammiel from Lo Debar. Barzillai would now find out mentoring the men had been worth his time and effort.

On that occasion, Barzillai forged the men into a team of Champions who took a chance by believing in a king who was God's man, but who had been humiliated by his prodigal son. Both had ample reason not to welcome David, but both became convinced that David was the one to believe in.

Barzillai, 80 years old, was a diplomat without a title, a good man with the balm of Gilead deeply rooted in his heart. He was a forgiver, a broker of peace, and a negotiator full of wisdom. He was the catalyst when a military coup and civil war were in play which involved none other than the King's own son, Absalom,[3] and conciliation seemed illusive and improbable.

Barzillai was a highlander[4] of the tribe of Manasseh. He lived in the town of Rogelim in the region known as Bashan, sometimes called the "Land of Gilead," the region of Gilead, Golan Heights, or simply Gilead. The acclaimed "Balm of Gilead"[5] had originated from his neighborhood and was eminent in the natural flavors of this man and his reputation.

The name Barzillai means "Man of Iron."[6] Without a doubt, this man was like an elder statesman, although he wasn't celebrated beyond his local highlands. To find him and recognize him for who he was, one had to travel east across the Jordan and climb up into the highlands. There it wouldn't be likely that people were talking about him, but you would discover that for some reason those hills had a different nature.

The Very Nature and Culture of the Highlands Produced Legends

The elites of this world misjudge the hearts and values of those who had their beginnings in the Highlands. Those who relate to the hinterlands, the hill countries, the cattle posts,[7] or the mountainous regions of most nations don't often boast of themselves or of the local sages their legends celebrate. Those places are often considered too remote at best. Some consider them to be primitive, backwater, middle of nowhere places which produce no one of great importance or national standing.

The elites are of the opinion that all the good stuff and notoriety originated in the urban areas. People in cities boast ever too freely of their gifts, their intellectual prowess, and their better ideas. And yet Barzillai did not come from a city of significance.

Contrary to the opinions of the elite, the regions of the world where men like Barzillai come from often produce the movers and shakers, both good and bad. Although city folks are central to national politics and dominate the local newscasts, it's often in the remote areas where more things are happening than meet the eye.

Barzillai was a hometown boy born and raised in Rogelim and in nearby Gilead. When he was young, he watched as adults collected the buds of cottonwood trees and processed them into what came to be known as the "Balm of Gilead." This balm was a rare perfume used medicinally.[8] It was named for the region in Gilead where it was produced[9] and is mentioned in the Bible. It was as if the essence of this balm was evident in Barzillai's nature. All who knew him viewed him as a man of peace, a gracious and forgiving man who went to great lengths to speak valuable life lessons into the lives of others.

BARZILLAI HAD BEEN BUSY MENTORING MEN LIKE SHOBI AND MACHIR LONG BEFORE KING DAVID ARRIVED.

Barzillai had formed many memories during his 80 years of life. He was born during Samuel's 46-year rule as Israel's last judge. Samuel had selected his own replacement by anointing Saul as Israel's first king. Although Samuel would continue as an elder statesman and the most prominent of Israel's priests for nearly all of Saul's 40 years as king, he would not often be in public view. When Saul became King, Barzillai was a teenager.

David was crowned King of Judah when Barzillai was nearly 50 years old. Seven years later, David was crowned King of Israel and ruled over all twelve tribes. When David was around 60 years old and had ruled Israel for about 31 years, Barzillai was an "octogenarian." It was then that Barzillai went to the aid of his King.

DO YOU ASPIRE TO BE AN INFLUENCER? IF YOU HOPE TO BE AN INFLUENCER IN A YEAR OR TWO, DON'T DELAY. START THE PROCESS TODAY.

Prince Shobi, Son of Nahash, from the Ammonite City of Rabbah

Please allow me to introduce you to the most unlikely member of this army of three, Shobi, the youngest son of the Ammonite king Nahash. Shobi's father had challenged the men of Jabesh-Gilead and threatened to gouge out their right eyes,[10] causing young Saul to rise and lead Israel to defend the city. That national crisis had catapulted Saul into his position as Israel's first king.[11]

PRINCE SHOBI WAS FROM A NEARBY NATION CALLED AMMON. HIS BROTHER WAS KING HANUN OF THE AMMONITES.

Shobi was obviously not Jewish, and many Hebrews probably considered him to be an enemy. He was stopped in his tracks when he was challenged by his friend, Barzillai.

Machir, Son of Ammiel, from Lo Debar

The second man mentored by Barzillai was Machir who had been biased against David because of his own issues. Machir had been a longtime friend of King Saul and his son, Jonathan, since they were all from the tribe of Benjamin. Abner had brought Jonathan's five-year-old son Mephibosheth to Machir after the death of his grandfather King Saul and his father Jonathan.[12] Mephibosheth's nurse had dropped him as they had fled the palace crippling him and causing him to need a special caregiver.[13]

MEPHIBOSHETH, SON OF PRINCE JONATHAN, HAD GROWN UP IN THE HOME OF MACHIR, A BENJAMITE.

Machir had merged Mephibosheth into his own family and had watched over and provided for him for over 20 years. After David befriended Mephibosheth and invited him to sit at his own family table, Machir realized David was a benevolent man.

SILHOUETTED ON THE HORIZON AGAINST THE EASTERN SKY ABOVE MAHANAIM WERE THREE MEN, LIKE CHAMPIONS, WHO HAD COME TO HELP DAVID:

BARZILLAI— THE GILEADITE FROM ROGELIM

PRINCE SHOBI— SON OF KING NAHASH, THE AMMONITE

MACHIR— THE CAREGIVER FOR MEPHIBOSHETH.

Barzillai, Prince Shobi, and Machir were all men of wealth and influence. They had not been trusting of David, but Barzillai's kind, gracious nature was the winning ticket. Barzillai and his team made an ally out of King David at a time when he desperately needed friends.

Barzillai bumped his leadership skills and influence up to a new level when he engaged and challenged Shobi and Machir to put aside their partisanship and stand for Israel's King in his distress. He successfully leveraged them to join him on a "mercy run" to take food and supplies to the King and his entourage and provide comfort and rest for them as they descended upon Mahanaim exhausted, hungry, and discouraged.

"When David arrived at Mahanaim, Prince Shobi, Machir, and Barzillai brought beds and blankets, bowls and jugs filled with wheat, barley, flour, roasted grain, beans and lentils, curds, cheese, honey, as well as flocks (of sheep) and herds (of cattle). They presented all this to David and his army to eat saying, 'the army must be starved and exhausted and thirsty out in this wilderness.'"[14]

The War Finally Ended and the Usurper Was Dead

The day came when news arrived by a runner[15] that the civil war was over and the main conspirator, Absalom,[16] had been slain by Joab in a battle at Gilead.

Since the war was over, Israel needed a leader. People from all over the nation sent word to David saying, "Return, you and all your servants!"[17] When David returned, leaders from Judah came and led the huge group of national leaders in welcoming the returning king. Many who had been verbally critical and hateful toward David arrived with totally changed attitudes. Shimei came in a fully repentant posture.[18]

Mephibosheth came later and reported to David how he had been misrepresented by the lies told by his servant Ziba. David then realized that Mephibosheth had not ceased being grateful for the kindness he had always shown to him.[19]

As David headed to the water's edge on the east side of the Jordan, he found a great contingency of followers. Half of Israel was rallying to welcome him and to travel back to the capital city of Jerusalem. With all the tribes gathered, they were determined to welcome the King and assist him in crossing the water. Some called their effort a "ferry."[20] Josephus wrote, "All these, as well as the tribe of Judah, laid a bridge (of boats) over the river that the King, and all those that were with him, might with ease pass over it."[21]

Barzillai came down from Rogelim as soon as he heard the civil war was over, prepared to join in the King's departure from the Eastern Plateau. He had planned to journey with David to Jordan and cross with him to the western side of that great river. The thoughts of his heart were to finish the job he had begun.

When Barzillai arrived at Jordan, David turned to his aging friend to thank him for providing for him and his compatriots throughout that short chapter of his life. Before David stepped onto the ferry, he said to Barzillai, "Come across with me, and I will provide for you while you are with me in Jerusalem."

Barzillai replied with these words:

> *"How many years do I have left that I should go up with the king to Jerusalem? I am now 80 years old. Do I know what is good or bad anymore? Can I taste what I eat or drink? Can I hear the voices of men or women singers? Why should your servant be a burden to his master and King? I will cross a short way over the Jordan with you, but why should the King give me such a reward? Let your servant return so I may die in my own town near the grave of my parents."*[22] *Please dismiss me, as I am already thinking of my end."*

IT WAS NO ACCIDENT THAT
BARZILLAI TOOK HIS YOUNGEST
SON CHIMHAM WITH HIM TO
BID DAVID GOODBYE WHEN HE
WAS READY TO CROSS JORDAN.

ALTHOUGH THE KING HAD MET
CHIMHAM EARLIER, THAT BECAME
A MOMENT TO REMEMBER!

Barzillai's conversation then transitioned to another level as he said to David,

> 'But here is your servant (my son) Chimham (pronounced: Kim'- ham);
>
> Let him cross over with my lord the king,
>
> and do for him what seems good to you.' [23]
>
> And the king answered: 'I will dismiss you, Barzillai,
>
> but please grant me your son, Chimham,
>
> and upon him I will bestow all sorts of good things.' [24]

It was a delicate moment for both David and Barzillai. David was speaking out of gratefulness for Barzillai's kindness, while Barzillai was keen to respect the heart intent of the King's wishes. At the same time, Barzillai carefully considered what response would be the wisest. After all, he wouldn't live much longer, and his son Chimham could carry the day into a stronger future.[25]

Barzillai chose to practice restraint and give his son to serve the King as his emissary. By not cashing in on David's obviously generous nature, Barzillai showed he trusted God to deal appropriately with the King. He trusted that David might choose to be even more generous with Chimham, if he himself showed restraint.

WHEN YOUR HEART IS ALIGNED WITH THE HOLY SPIRIT AND YOU DEPEND ON HIS "STILL SMALL VOICE" TO HELP YOU IN YOUR CHOICES, IT WILL MAKE ALL THE DIFFERENCE IN THE WORLD!

BARZILLAI LISTENED TO HIS HEART!

Chapter 6

DAVID SEARCHES HIS SOUL

He Considers His Adopted Son, Chimham

Jordan was behind him, and his journey home was in progress as David moved from the western bank of the Jordan River toward the capital city of Jerusalem. On the journey, he had been able to deal with some disgruntled individuals. Others, however, would continue to "dog" him in the months and years to come. Absalom was dead, and the war had ended, but life for David and the nation of Israel would continue to be a struggle to achieve a degree of normalcy.

A new challenge faced the nation because a different mood prevailed within many of the people. They were having a difficult time overcoming the doubt that Absalom[1] had planted in their hearts through his attempt to usurp the throne of his father, David. Men like Sheba had risen up and created civil unrest,[2] and chaos dominated the land as usurper after usurper carved away at the nation's fabric. After a while the chaos became so deep it almost turned to anarchy.

It took some time for the nation to settle down after suffering such great trauma. Families had been negatively activated and unsettled by doubt. The anarchy continued for a number of years, and unfortunately, it appeared that the Kingdom had crumbled in many ways.

During his early reign, David had been the nation's favorite son and admired King. People had loved him and his family and also his mighty men and the strength they had represented. After the Coup d'état ended, David settled back into family life and began to re-establish the politics of the nation.

David Takes Inventory

King David eventually began to take inventory. He looked back over his past high-points and low-points and tried to make sense of them all. He looked less and less at the dark memories and more and more at the happier moments.

He longed for the counsel of Barzillai, but since that was no longer available, he pushed forward by searching his own soul. He wanted to repay Barzillai for his kindness, generosity, and hospitality. Since in his heart he had adopted Barzillai's son Chimham and viewed him as one of his own sons, he began to ask himself, "How can I bless Chimham and bring a lasting and greater honor to my old friend?"[3]

David had clear memories of his own childhood on the hillsides surrounding Bethlehem. At times he longed to relive life by recreating some of those happier childhood moments. Perhaps he thought if he reflected on his memories and appealed to his heart to live more righteously, he would make fewer mistakes in the future.

WHEN YOU MUST COME UP WITH A SOLUTION TO A DILEMMA, YOU NEED DIVINE WISDOM. SOUL SEARCHING IS A HELPFUL PART OF THE PROCESS.

He remembered how delighted he'd been when his parents had bequeathed the old homestead to him. He still possessed that treasure, but through the years he had done nothing with it. It had been a long time since he'd even visited Bethlehem. But although he was living in a palace in the city of Jerusalem, he realized his inheritance from Jesse was his most valuable personal possession.

David longed for the simple life of Bethlehem as he thought back to the land and the love and warmth he'd enjoyed there. He reminisced about when he had watched his sheep on that land and the surrounding hills. And he thought about the people in his past. He had first experienced the love of his family and the love of his God there. He remembered playing his harp and raising his voice to sing praises to God while he watched his sheep on the hillsides. That lifestyle had eventually caused all of Israel to refer to him as "the Sweet Psalmist of Israel."

While watching sheep, David had also called to remembrance oral history that had been passed down to him about his ancestors.

He remembered hearing that his great-great-grandfather Salmon had received their family land from Joshua as his portion of the land that was divided up when Israel took possession of Canaan. Salmon had then married Rahab, a Canaanite harlot who had lived in a house on the wall of the city of Jericho. She had befriended the two spies who were searching out the land before the invasion by Israel. Some people felt that Salmon had been one of the two spies[4] sent out by Joshua to Jericho, but that hasn't been proven. It was amazing to David that he could proudly think of Rahab in a good light as his great-great-grandmother.[5]

After Salmon married Rahab, they began a long history that continued generation after generation. Their son Boaz was born on the land, and there Boaz had met and married Ruth. Obed, the son of Boaz and Ruth, was the father of Jesse, David's father. David realized his family had become famous and had been blessed by God in many ways. "He [God] always stands by his covenant—the commitment he made to a thousand generations."[6]

During one of the moments when David was reminiscing, a brilliant idea formed in his mind. He thought, "I know what I can do for Chimham. I can pass my own inheritance to him by giving him one of my most precious possessions. I will give him my childhood home in honor of his father, my old friend Barzillai."[7]

Whatever the process David experienced that day that helped him come to that viable solution is not important. The important thing is that David gave his childhood family home to Chimham. Perhaps he thought that would be a brilliant way to help Chimham create a happy place where he could enjoy life, raise his family, and perhaps make his own dreams come true. And so, David entrusted to Chimham the stewardship of his family inheritance, and Chimham became the recipient of David's goodness and generosity.

David didn't know what Chimham would do with the property, but he was assured in his heart that the young man would use it wisely, carefully, and responsibly. Through his generosity, David felt assured that his own family would be highly honored and expanded. After making his decision, all he had to do was inform Chimham that he intended to invest in him, and that the investment was for the future and in honor of Barzillai.

The Scenario That Apparently Developed over the Years

The first thing Chimham did was relocate his family to Bethlehem. He then transformed his property into a hub of hospitality for his family, friends, and travelers who would pass through from Bashan. We don't know if David ever visited, but we expect that word would have come to him that reminded him of happier days and Barzillai's wonderful hospitality. David surely smiled as he imagined Chimham and his wife and children, and perhaps even merchants and friends from his own childhood, who enjoyed their visits and appreciated the kindness shown by the warmth emanating from the Inn. It's apparent that Barzillai's "acts of kindness" toward David became a blessing he would never forget.

Not long before his death, King David expressed his heart to Solomon saying, "If you wish to gratify me and honor me, your father, then you must take greater care of Chimham for what his father did for me when I was in flight from your brother, Absalom." In his heart David was saying, "We have only done the minimum for him, in that we have only paid the debt we owed."[8]

71

A Busy Caravansary [kar-uh-van-suh-ree]

It appears that Chimham transformed the ancestral home of David first into his own home, then into a compound, then into an inn, and finally into a caravansary.[9] The caravansary accommodated the many merchant-led camel and donkey caravans[10] that crisscrossed the land taking items to markets in the north and south.[11] The ancestral home where David grew up no longer served only one family. It had become a place of hospitality for friends and strangers alike.

THE CHILDHOOD HOME OF KING DAVID BECAME THE VERY PLACE WHERE JESUS WAS BORN!

Eventually, Joseph and Mary arrived at the Inn seeking a place for Mary to give birth to Jesus. There was "no room that night inside the Inn,"[12] but there was a grotto on the property where the sheep and other animals were kept. That became the place where Mary birthed Jesus and laid him in a manger.

All Christians have appreciated the fact that Jesus was the Messiah who came through Judah and eventually through David. However, many may not have realized that Jesus was born on the very same property where David had been born.

IT'S WORTHY TO NOTE
THAT JESUS IS CALLED THE
"SON OF DAVID." THEY HAD
THE SAME ANCESTRY AND
WERE BOTH BORN ON THE
SAME PIECE OF LAND.

So, all the generations from Abraham to David are fourteen generations; and from David until the carrying away into Babylon are fourteen generations; and from the carrying away into Babylon unto Christ are fourteen generations.[13]

There was a strong connection between David and Jesus, the "Son of David." According to history, there were 28 generations separating them, with David being Jesus' grandfather many times over. The reason the Bible focuses on David out of all the forefathers is because of the covenant God made with him. It was known as the Davidic Covenant, and it assured David that the Messiah would come as one of his descendants.[14]

Over a thousand years later, Jesus, his disciples, and a huge group of followers were leaving Jericho. Bartimaeus, a blind beggar, realized the crowd passing him was following Jesus. He was aware of the connection between David and Jesus because of a common rumor which ran throughout the grassroots culture of Israel. Knowing he might never again have an opportunity to encounter Jesus, Bartimaeus loudly, desperately, and repeatedly called out to Jesus. This is the account from the New Testament book of Mark:

Then they reached Jericho, and as Jesus and his disciples left town, a large crowd followed him. A blind beggar named Bartimaeus (son of Timaeus) was sitting beside the road. When Bartimaeus heard that Jesus of Nazareth was nearby, he began to shout, "Jesus, Son of David, have mercy on me!" "Be quiet!" many of the people yelled at him. But he only shouted louder, "Son of David, have mercy on me!"

When Jesus heard the man calling, he stopped and said, "Tell him to come here." So they told the blind man, "Cheer up and come. He's calling you!" Bartimaeus threw off his coat, jumped up, and hurried to Jesus.

"What do you want me to do for you?" Jesus asked. "My Rabbi," the blind man said, "I want to see!" And Jesus said to him, "Go, for your faith has healed you." Instantly the man could see, and he followed Jesus down the road.[15]

The Almighty God has always gone to great lengths to make His plans come together for his people. David's loyalty to an elderly statesman for his acts of kindness 3,000 years ago are a great inspiration to us today. We are still intrigued by all that happened as a result of it.

Chapter 7

A PROPHETIC CONNECTION

The Prophet Jeremiah's Stay at the Inn in Bethlehem

Many who are interested in the "place where Jesus was born" will be inspired when they realize that even during the time of the "Exile" God blessed His people with rest on David's family's farm where he had grown up. God always honored His promise concerning the coming Messiah.

Israel's history had progressed 400 years past the days of David before Jeremiah the prophet came on the scene. This prominent seer lived in Israel during the days of Nebuchadnezzar's invasion of the nation. The historical setting during that period was Jerusalem before the Babylonian invasion of 597 BC.

Before Nebuchadnezzar's first invasion, Jeremiah sounded a national alert to the Israelites that war was facing them, and they would be defeated. His prophetic word declared to everyone from King Zedekiah to the poorest farmer that their government had been in rebellion against God and would face their day of reckoning. He told them if they would repent immediately, God, who was full of grace and mercy, would forgive them. He urged them to take the warning seriously because Nebuchadnezzar would not be as forgiving as God.[1] Jeremiah's final warning was that if their national repentance wasn't sincere, they were doomed to defeat by the Babylonians.

Jeremiah Prophesied God's Judgement

Jeremiah saw the future by the spirit and prophesied that God was sending the Babylonians to judge Israel. The Israelites were told to yield to the enemy if they wanted mercy. If they didn't obey, Nebuchadnezzar, king of Babylon, would defeat, destroy, and humiliate all of Israel, as well as other nations in the region. From the throne of Heaven, God declared,

> *And now I have given all these lands into the hand of Nebuchadnezzar the king of Babylon, my servant; and the beasts of the field I have also given him to serve him.*[2]

Jeremiah boldly told the national leaders and the people of Israel they would soon go into captivity, but that after 70 years they would return to their homeland for a full restoration and to rebuild Jerusalem. Daniel and many young members of the royal family had already been taken to Babylon as captives in 605 BC.

Although Jeremiah prophesied loudly, clearly, and forcefully, he was met with strong reprisal. He then made an oxen's yoke, placed it around his own neck, and walked the streets in protest of the nation's unrepentant nature. When the kings of the neighboring nations—Edom, Moab, Ammon, Tyre, and Sidon—sent their ambassadors to visit King Zedekiah, Jeremiah sent messages back with them to their home countries to warn them that they were going to suffer the same fate as Israel.[3]

The King and most of his court officials were furious with Jeremiah, and the King immediately sent for him. All types of accusations were made against Jeremiah. They included the questioning of his loyalty and patriotism, since in effect, he was urging the nation to raise a white flag in surrender. He told them if they refused to repent *en masse*, they had to surrender or their nation would be burnt to the ground. Instead of heeding Jeremiah's warning, they immediately took the prophet into custody and cast him into the dungeon where the King's guard was housed.

> *So, the officials took Jeremiah from his cell and lowered him by ropes into an empty cistern in the prison yard. It belonged to Malkijah, a member of the royal family. There was no water in the cistern, but there was a thick layer of mud at the bottom, and Jeremiah sank down into it.*

The mud was like quicksand,[4] so Jeremiah sank into it. Within a few days, he was badly dehydrated and on the verge of starvation.

An Ethiopian Eunuch Saves Jeremiah's Life

Ebed-Melech, a Cushite from Ethiopia, was a court official that had roots that likely reached back to the days of the Queen of Sheba and forward to those who would in later years be called "Coptic."[5] He was a man with a compassionate heart and became sympathetic toward Jeremiah when he saw what was done to him.

Ebed-Melech greatly respected Jeremiah and regularly checked on him. He appealed to King Zedekiah to have the prophet released, but Zedekiah was politically weak and unwilling to help. Finally, after repeated appeals, the King yielded and gave the Cushite permission to do whatever he wished to rescue the prophet. The appeal to the King had been so convincing that he ordered 30 men to assist Ebed-Melech in his rescue operation.[6] It's impressive that on that day, the court official took a higher rank and became a commander for a special assignment.

Ebed-Melech directed the soldiers to collect old rags and clothes. They wrapped them around ropes and slipped the ropes under Jeremiah's arms so that in his weakened and dehydrated state he would not be further injured as they pulled him from the cistern. The rescue reflected kindness and mercy from the heart. After Jeremiah was pulled from the well and given water and food, the soldiers transferred him to the prison to prevent him from escaping.

While Jeremiah was in prison and the second invasion was just beginning, the Lord spoke a clear word to him. God told him to go to the house of Ebed-Melech the Ethiopian and say, "Although God will bring this city down, you will be set free. You will not fall into the hands of those you fear."[7] In that way, God showed grace and mercy to Ebed-Melech for saving Jeremiah's life.

During the second invasion, Nebuchadnezzar fully briefed his military captain Nebuzaradan and sent him with his armies to deal with the chaos and trouble in Israel. It was clear that King Nebuchadnezzar had been getting constant updates from his officials and spies in the land, and he was aware there had been an uprising after his first invasion. He was also informed that there was a prophet by the name of Jeremiah who had been declaring essentially these words:

Israel, you and your leaders have been walking in rebellion
against God and now will come to calamity. I will send my
army of Babylon to bring you to judgment. As I send them,
they will not be as merciful and as forgiving as I have been.
My advice is to surrender to their King, or you will die.

When Babylon's king received the news of Jeremiah's prophetic words, he was pleased. He felt empowered by the fact that Israel's God was on his side. He then gave direct and personal instructions to Nebuzaradan to line the Israelites up, chain them together, and march them out of their country and to the land of Babylon. Nebuchadnezzar further instructed Nebuzaradan to search for the old prophet Jeremiah and release him from Zedekiah's custody.

After Nebuzaradan captured the city of Jerusalem and secured control of the nation, he inspected all the prisoners. He walked straight down the line calling, "Where are you, Jeremiah?" Finally, someone answered, "He is here. Jeremiah is here."

When Jeremiah stepped out of the line, the military captain said, "Release this man and let him go." Then he said, "Jeremiah, it's obvious you have spoken the truth. See how I am setting you free from the chains that were on your hands. You are free to choose. Go with me to Babylon as my guest, and I will provide for you, or stay here in your land. Wherever you choose, you are free to go."

Jeremiah said, "I want to remain here in Israel with my people."[8] Nebuzaradan granted the old prophet freedom to go with the impoverished people of the land. He then gave him food and a gift and let him go.

Only the poorest Jews were left behind in Judah to grow crops and tend the land. King Nebuchadnezzar appointed Gedaliah to serve as his Jewish tributary or governor over the region. It was common for a conquered people to be given a governor from among their own to serve as a representative between Babylon and the locals. Some Chaldean soldiers also remained in the land to keep order and ensure no rebellion took place. Gedaliah served as governor from the town of Mizpah which was north of Jerusalem. When those who had fled from the invaders heard that Gedaliah had been established as governor, they returned to Judah. Among those who returned were several groups of soldiers who had not been in Jerusalem during the siege and had not been captured. As they arrived, Gedaliah wisely urged everyone to accept their fate and live at peace in the land under the rule of the Babylonians. They had nothing left to fear. The Chaldeans would not harm them if they remained peaceful. "Gedaliah assured the officers and their men, giving them his word, 'Don't be afraid of the Babylonian officials. Go back to your farms and families and respect the king of Babylon. Trust me, everything is going to be all right.'"[9]

Jeremiah went to live near Gedaliah in Mizpah, the new seat of government. Since his voice was a voice from the Lord, he probably felt being near the seat of government would be best. The nation began to prosper and flourish, and there was a general optimism in the hearts of the people because they felt more comfortable with Gedaliah's leadership than they had with Zedekiah's.[10]

There was, however, an uneasiness forming in the minds of those who had agendas, such as Ishmael, a wicked man with personal agendas. He didn't have the character to be a good leader because he was a man with war in his spirit. He had a small army of men who had remained loyal to him as their commander and had been hiding out in Ammon with him.

Ishmael had a heart much like Absalom and had elevated himself to the position of a "warlord." He felt he had to rise up and lead as a judge would have done during the time of the Judges. A conspiracy was growing, and word of it leaked to Johanan, a Jewish soldier with soldiers under him who stood with Gedaliah.

Johanan, who had a good heart and was supportive of Gedaliah and what he was doing to bring about a stable government, warned Gedaliah of Ishmael's threat. Johanan offered to slip into Ishmael's camp and kill him, so no one would know, and Gedaliah would be safe to lead. However, Gedaliah refused to believe him, thinking Ishmael was incapable of such treachery.[11]

Thirty days passed, and Gedaliah held a feast. He invited Ishmael to join the celebration. Ishmael arrived accompanied by ten of his men. Gedaliah invited them in, and the scene drastically changed as the ambitious Ishmael carried out his evil plan. During the feast, the ruthless band attacked and slew Gedaliah. Having assassinated their host, they then commenced to massacre many prominent followers of Gedaliah and put to the sword the small Chaldean garrison stationed at Mizpah.[12] His murderous deed accomplished, Ishmael left Mizpah with many captives and headed for Ammon.[13]

Johanan heard the news of the massacre and rallied his men and several other small armies. They pursued the criminals to Gibeon, a short distance away, and succeeded in rescuing the captives; but Ishmael and eight of his men escaped and fled across the border into Ammon.[14]

Next Stop, the Inn at Bethlehem

Johanan now faced another dilemma, since he was leading a small multitude of men, women, children, dignitaries, soldiers, and eunuchs from Mizpah. He feared their noise would awaken the Babylonians, and King Nebuchadnezzar would be furious and destroy them. Therefore, he decided they should find refuge in Egypt. Jeremiah, who had been taken on the journey against his will, was facing spending his last days in Egypt.

Johanan and the refugees needed a place to rest, regroup, and plan their strategy, and the well-known Inn at Bethlehem was right on their way. Johanan steered his entourage to the site of King David's inheritance, still bearing the name of Chimham to whom David had given the land in honor of Chimham's father Barzillai.[15]

AUTHOR'S NOTE:

IT WAS OBVIOUS TO JEREMIAH THAT DAVID HAD GIVEN THE LAND TO CHIMHAM BECAUSE 400 YEARS AFTER CHIMHAM HAD PASSED AWAY, THE LAND WAS STILL KNOWN AS THE "HABITATION OF CHIMHAM."

There, four centuries earlier, Chimham had built a home of hospitality which continued to be available for weary travelers.[16]

In those days, guest houses were not common, but Chimham's dwelling place or Inn had a special historical significance as a "House of Bread."[17] It had taken a number of years for the Inn to develop, but it had grown and continued until the days of Jeremiah.[18] Johanan, his small army, Jeremiah, the other refugees, and possibly donkeys, horses and camels all found rest in that unique caravansary.

"AND THEY WENT AND STAYED IN GERUTH [THE LODGING PLACE OF] CHIMHAM, WHICH IS NEAR BETHLEHEM, INTENDING TO GO TO EGYPT."

JEREMIAH 41:17 AMP

Johanan the son of Kareah and all the commanders of the forces that were with him took from Mizpah all the people whom he had rescued from Ishmael the son of Nethaniah after Ishmael had killed Gedaliah (the governor appointed by Nebuchadnezzar) the son of Ahikam, the soldiers, the women, the children, and the high officials whom Johanan had brought back from Gibeon. And they went and stayed in Geruth [the lodging place of] Chimham, which is near Bethlehem, intending to go to Egypt.[19]

EPILOGUE

The concluding question and answer:

What makes the place where Jesus was born so significant?
The person of Jesus Christ Himself

God accomplished "redemption" through the coming of Jesus Christ. His birth was foretold, He came to earth, and He lived a sinless life. He then stood firmly in the halls of the Roman government resolved to offer Himself to ruthless, godless men who would torture and crucify Him. On that cross, Jesus became the "Passover Lamb," the sacrifice for the sins of the entire world.

Whether you embrace that offering and His sacrifice and receive your redemption is entirely up to you. Some say, "There is no God." God's reply is, "Only a fool would say, 'There is no God!'"[1]

Some say, "If God really existed, He would stop the evil in this world and give us only the good things that make our lives more pleasant and pain free." My response is, "Before Jesus stopped to heal the blind eyes of Bartimaeus, Bartimaeus had to "call out to Jesus and ask for his healing."[2]

Many men and women in their heart of hearts stubbornly refuse to bend their knees in repentance and humility and say, "Please Lord Jesus, heal me and forgive me for the evil in my heart and for my sins." Jeremiah 17:9 says it best, "The heart is deceitful above all things and desperately wicked, who can know it."[3]

The only way to eliminate evil from your life is to repent and believe on the Lord Jesus Christ. He will then transform your life by sending the Holy Spirit to heal your soul. At that moment you will be forgiven of your sins and will experience the new birth—be "born again."[4]

As long as the people around you continue on the wide road of sin, they will do evil things. However, you can change your own life and future by changing your eternal destination. Bartimaeus' eyes wouldn't have been healed if he hadn't called out to Jesus saying, "Have mercy on me." Evil will continue in this world as long as people foolishly and stubbornly refuse to bend their knees to the Lord Jesus Christ.

Epilogue

A Call to Repentance

Dr. Billy Graham gave wonderful calls to repentance as he preached to countless millions in 185 nations and territories around the world. It has been estimated that 2.2 billion people heard him preach in person.[5] The following is one of those infamous calls to repentance:

> *"Repentance means you change your mind about God, about yourself, and about your need.*
>
> *When you change your mind, Christ transforms it. We've all sinned, and that's the reason God sent Jesus Christ to die on the cross.*
>
> *What do you have to do? You have to be willing to repent of your sins. That means you have to be willing to change your mind, your heart, and your attitude and pray, "Lord, I've sinned, and I'm sorry."*
>
> *It means you're willing to ask God to help you turn from your sin and change your way of living.*
>
> *That's repentance.*
>
> *Change your mind, and He'll change your heart!*
>
> *Change your heart, and He'll come in and regenerate you.*
>
> *You will become a born again person.*
>
> *Don't wait!*
>
> *Today is the day of salvation. Come to Jesus now."[6]*

How Old Was Jesus When the Wise Men Came?[1]

By Ray Geide

It seems that every Christmas someone—a pastor, a friend, or a teacher—insists that the Nativity scenes and the common Christmas story are all wrong because Jesus had to have been a toddler by the time the Wise Men arrived in Bethlehem. Is this Biblical? Once and for all, I would like to answer the question, "How old was Jesus when the Wise Men came?"

There are two opposing viewpoints. The traditional view is that Jesus was a baby. I call this view the Wise Men/Baby Jesus View. The other view says Jesus was one or two years old. I call this view the Wise Men/Toddler Jesus View.

The Wise Men/Toddler Jesus View

The Wise Men/Toddler Jesus View seems to have it roots in the actions of King Herod at the time of Jesus' birth. When the Wise Men came to him looking for the Messiah, he asked them when the star had appeared. (Matthew 2:7)

The Wise Men went to visit Jesus and then returned to their homes. When Herod saw they had not returned to him as he had asked them to, he "was exceeding wroth, and sent forth, and slew all the children that were in Bethlehem, and in all the coasts thereof, from two years old and under, according to the time which he had diligently enquired of the Wise Men," (Matthew 2:16 KJV). Evidently, Herod figured Jesus had to have been born around the time when the star had appeared or later.

The Wise Men/Toddler Jesus crowd agree with Herod's conclusion. They make three points in support of their view:

1. Jesus was born when the star appeared.

2. Jesus is called a young child, not a baby, in the Wise Men account. (Matthew 2:8-9, 11, 13-14, 20-21 KJV)

3. The Wise Men found Jesus in a house, not a stable or an inn. (Matthew 2:11)

These points may sound plausible, but upon closer examination of the Bible and its underlying Greek text, some major problems emerge.

How Old Was Jesus When the Wise Men Came?

"Now when Jesus was born in Bethlehem of Judaea in the days of Herod the king, behold, there came Wise Men from the east to Jerusalem." (KJV) This verse states that the Wise Men came to Jerusalem "when Jesus was born," (Matthew 2:1). They did not come a year later. They came when he was born.

The Star's Beginning

The Bible does not say Jesus was born when the star first appeared. Those who say He was are only guessing.

Despite who Herod was, he didn't know when Jesus was born. Just because he ordered that children two years old and under should be killed does not mean that Jesus was two years old at that time. Herod evidently thought Jesus could also have been a newborn baby because he ordered all children under two to be killed.

A Baby Is Also Called a Young Child

The Greek word behind the term "young child" is *paidion*. It doesn't refer only to a toddler. It may also refer to a newborn baby. *Paidion* was used concerning John the Baptist when he was eight days old. (Luke 1:59, 66, 76, 80)

The term was also used concerning Jesus when he was born (Luke 2:17), when he was eight days old (Luke 2:21), and when he was 40 days old (Luke 2:27, 40). In fact, *paidion* was used concerning Jesus when the shepherds were at the manger on the night of Jesus' birth, only one verse after babe *(brephos)* is used. (Luke 2:17) So just because Jesus is called a young child *(paidion)* in the Wise Men account in Matthew, doesn't mean he was older than a baby.

The Wise Men Arrived in Jerusalem When Jesus Was Born

Another proof for the Wise Men/Baby Jesus View is Matthew 2:1. "Now when Jesus was born in Bethlehem of Judaea in the days of Herod the king, behold, there came Wise Men from the east to Jerusalem." (KJV) That verse states that the Wise Men came to Jerusalem "when Jesus was born." They did not come a year later. They came when he was born.

"When Jesus was born" is an aorist participle in Greek. It can be translated as "when Jesus was born," "after Jesus was born, or "Jesus was born and." Aorist participles are frequent in the New Testament. With an aorist participle, the action of the participle (Jesus was born) is closely followed by the action of the main verb (Wise Men came to Jerusalem). There was not a year or two or even a week or two between the time Jesus was born and when the Wise Men came to Jerusalem.

Bethlehem was only half a day's walk from Jerusalem. It didn't take the Wise Men long to get to Bethlehem after they'd arrived in Jerusalem when Jesus was born.

We Know When Joseph and Mary Returned to Nazareth

Another proof for the Wise Men/Baby Jesus View is the return of Joseph, Mary, and Jesus back to Nazareth. It only happened once, and both the Wise Men account (Matthew) and the shepherd account (Luke) record it. In the shepherd account, it's clear that Mary, Joseph, and Jesus returned to Nazareth very close to 40 days after Jesus was born, (Luke 2:39) "when the days of her purification according to the law of Moses were accomplished," (Luke 2:22). The

Wise Men account tells us that they returned to Nazareth after their return from Egypt (Matthew 2:22-23). So, the Wise Men's visit, Joseph and Mary's trip to Egypt, and the Wise Men's trip home all had to have happened within 40 days of Jesus' birth.

The Christmas Timeline

- The Wise Men entered Jerusalem and asked where the Messiah was.

- Herod asked the scribes who hand copied the Old Testament where the new king would be born. They answered, "In Bethlehem."

- Herod asked the Wise Men to find the Messiah and come back and tell him where he was.

- The Wise Men traveled to Bethlehem in the cool of the night. The star reappeared and guided the Wise Men to the house where Jesus was. The Wise Men went into the house and gave Jesus gifts.

- As the Wise Men slept that night, God warned them in a dream not to return to Herod but to go home a different way. They obeyed the warning.

- The next night an angel appeared to Joseph in a dream and told him to take his family and escape to Egypt.

- Joseph, Mary and Jesus traveled to Egypt.

- Herod saw that the Wise Men had not returned. He became angry and had all the children in Bethlehem that were two years old and younger killed.

- Joseph, Mary, and Jesus stayed in Egypt for about a month.

- Herod died.

* Again, an angel appeared to Joseph in a dream. The angel told him it was alright to return to Israel. Joseph, Mary and Jesus traveled to Jerusalem. They went to the temple to offer the sacrifices required by the law. Simeon and Anna recognized baby Jesus as the Messiah.

How old was Jesus when the Wise Men came? The Bible doesn't say exactly how old He was; but from what it does say, we can make a safe guess that He was from just born to several days old. He was not one or two years old.

ENDNOTES

Chapter 1
THE BIRTH OF JOHN THE BAPTIST

Endnotes

1. https://www.biblestudytools.com/bible-study/topical-studies/what-is-the-meaning-of-bc-and-ad-what-does-jesus-have-to-do-with-it.html ~ What Do BC and AD Mean? While most believe AD stands for after death, it actually comes from the Latin phrase "anno domini" which means "year of our Lord." Dionysius believed, perhaps rightly, that history should be divided by the greatest event in human history; namely, the birth of Jesus Christ. Thus all time after the birth of Christ became known as AD and all of history before the birth of Christ was labeled BC for "before Christ."

2. Religious Educator Vol. 14 No. 2 · 2013 ~ The most frequently occurring personal name in the Bible is Zechariah (also spelled Zachariah or in the New Testament as Zacharias). At least thirty kings, princes, priests, prophets, servants, sons, trumpet players, and gatekeepers claim this name, which means "Jehovah remembers." Some versions of the NT stick with the OT spelling, but in this book, we prefer to use Zacharias consistently.

3. Isaiah 40 especially v. 3 (Read the entire chapter to see the full prophecy.)

4. John 1:23 NKJV ~ John was quoting from Isaiah 40:3, which says: "The voice of one crying in the wilderness: 'Prepare the way of the Lord: make straight in the desert a highway for our God.'"

5. 1 Samuel 9:9 NKJV ~ Formerly in Israel when a man went to inquire of God, he spoke thus: "Come, let us go to the seer." for he who is now called a prophet was formerly called a seer.

6. Daniel 4:13 NKJV ~ "I saw in the visions of my head while on my bed, and there was a watcher, a holy one, coming down from heaven."

7. https://www.gotquestions.org/angel-Gabriel.html - The angel Gabriel is a messenger who was entrusted to deliver several important messages on God's behalf. Gabriel appears to at least three people in the Bible: first to the prophet Daniel (Daniel 8:16); next to the priest Zechariah to foretell and announce the miraculous birth of John the Baptist (Luke 1:19); and finally to the Virgin Mary to tell her that she would conceive and bear a son. (Luke 1:26–38) Gabriel's name means "God is great," and as the angel of the annunciation, he is the one who revealed that the Savior was to be called "Jesus."

8. https://www.answers.com/Q/How_far_is_Jerusalem_from_Nazareth

9. Luke 1:12 NLT

10. Luke 1:18 NLT

11. https://www.biblegateway.com/passage - Luke 1:5-2:20 GW - The Angel Gabriel Appeared to Zacharias "...So it was, that while he was serving as priest before God in the order of his division, according to the custom of the priesthood, his lot fell to burn incense when he went into the temple of the Lord. And the whole multitude of the people were praying outside at the hour of incense. Then an angel of the Lord appeared to him, standing on the right side of the altar of incense. And when Zacharias saw him, he was troubled, and fear fell upon him."

12. Luke 1:25 NLT

13. The bride price (mnēsteuō in Greek) is a sum of money or quantity of goods given to a bride's family by that of the groom, especially in tribal societies.

14. According to the Mishnah Ketubbot 5.2, the betrothal would generally last a year, with the bride remaining in the home of her father. Source: Douglas Stuart, Hosea-Jonah, Word Biblical Commentary, vol. 31 (Waco, TX: Word Books, 1987), p. 59.

15. www.blueletterbible.org/lang/lexicon/lexicon.cfm?t=kjv&strongs=g3423 - "To woo her and ask her in marriage: Passive response: to be promised in marriage, to be betrothed. Matthew 1:18, Luke 1:27, Luke 2:5. In other words, that means the marriage cannot be sexually consummated until the official ceremony has taken place.

16. Quote from Movie: "The Nativity Story". A comment made by the man who played Mary's father.

17. Luke 1:28 NKJV

18. Luke 1:35-37 CEV

19. https://earlychurchhistory.org/politics/john-the-baptist-his-birth-place/ - Today the village considered to be the home of Zacharias and Elizabeth is called: Ein Karem. When John was born, it was called Beth Hakerem (meaning "House of the Vineyard") and stood just outside of Jerusalem.

20. Luke 1:41-45 CEV

21. Luke 1:56

22. https://carm.org/what-was-the-subject-of-John-the-Baptists-preaching ~ by Luke Wayne ~ "John the Baptist preached a message of repentance expressed in water baptism and bearing active fruit in one's life in preparation for the appearing of the Messiah, whose coming would represent a divine visitation; the very presence of God coming to His people. In other words, he preached the essential gospel message of repentance resulting from faith in Jesus as the divine Messiah."

23. Mark 1:1-3 MSG

Chapter 2
THE BIRTH OF JESUS, THE CHRIST

Endnotes

1. There is historical evidence of men who were miraculously raised from the dead: I Kings 17:21-22, II Kings 4:35.

2. II Kings 5 gives us the story of Naaman, who was healed of leprosy after obeying the prophet Elisha and washing in the muddy Jordan. "

3. Matthew 1:18-25 CEB

4. Not clothes (like shirts, or slacks, etc.) but strips of cloth. The purpose is to restrict the infant from moving so as to create a sense of warmth and security ~ https://en.wikipedia. org/wiki/ Swaddling ~ Swaddling is an age-old practice of wrapping infants in blankets or similar cloths so that movement of the limbs is tightly restricted. Swaddling bands were often used to further restrict the infant.

5. Luke 2:1-7 NKJV

6. www.latimes.com/archives/la-xpm-1995-12-23-me-17102-story.html ~ A Long, Cold Road to Bethlehem: Nativity: Gospel accounts of Mary and Joseph's journey gloss over the arduous reality of life and travel in ancient Galilee, scholars say.

7. Luke 2:7 KJV The reason for the comment: "because there was no room for them in the inn," Is because there was historical proof that there was a traditional Inn in Bethlehem. This inn had been there back to the days of Jeremiah 41:7 and all the way back to the days of King David. This was actually on the site of where David grew up with his family. It was his inheritance which he had passed to Chimham as a gift. There was a physical grotto behind it where the sheep were kept.

8. Grotto: a naturally formed chamber or small cave. Often a grotto is nearly hidden from easy view, and with walls thick enough to create a cooler environment. In this case, the stable on the property they camped on for the night was a grotto, where its owners kept the sheep and other animals.

9. http://www.bibleprobe.com/bethlehem.htm ~ This account was reported to have been found in Constantinople archives. It shows that there was quite a "ruckus" during the night of Christ's birth. So much so that "all of Bethlehem" may have seen angels and/or night lights and heard angelic singing.

10. Luke 2:8-16 NKJV

11. Matthew 2:1-2 NKJV

12. https://www.merriam-webster.com/dictionary/astronomer ~ a person who is skilled in astronomy or who makes observations of celestial phenomena.

13. Britannica.com/topic/Magi

14. The Star over Bethlehem ~ Lots of research and many studies and evaluations have been made by scientists and astronomers through the centuries. These ideas have involved Comets, stars, planetary conjunctions (Jupiter, Saturn and Venus), eclipses, Supernovas. My aim is not to determine which has the most credibility, but merely to affirm that it came, was extremely bright, focused on a specific site, and stayed long enough to draw the attention of several visitors to the site of the Grotto and the Inn. Jesus, the Messiah aka the "King of the Jews," had come, and man must not miss the historical moment.

15. If you're interested in doing your own research re: the controversy of whether Jesus was an infant, or a toddler when the Magi came, begin at this site: https://strangenotions.com/the-100-year-old-mistake-about-the-birth-of-jesus ~ "The 100-Year Old Mistake About the Birth of Jesus", by Jimmy Akin. In the late 1800s, a German scholar named Emil Schürer proposed that Herod died earlier than previously thought. Specifically, he claimed that Herod died in 4 B.C. This view caught on among scholars, and so now it's common for people to date the birth of Jesus no later than 4 B.C. If a scholar takes seriously the account of the slaughter of the holy innocents then, since Herod killed all the baby boys two years old and under, that would push Jesus' birth up to two years earlier, landing us in 6 B.C. So that's why people often date Jesus' birth in this way, even though it is *not* when the Church Fathers indicated Jesus was born.

16. Refer to the Appendix: "How old was Jesus when the Magi came?"

17. www.Biblestudytools.com/dictionary/chimham ~ Jeremiah 41:17 This is often referred to as the Habitation of Chimham, or the Inn. This Inn was a place where hospitality was offered and was seen as probably an inn or khan, which is the proper meaning of the Hebrew "Geruth", rendered here as "habitation". Initially it had been given by King David to Chimham, the son of Barzillai. This will be dealt with later in the book.

18. Josephus Book 7, Chapter 11:4:274 - Barzillai begs leave of David and sends his son Chimham to accompany him to Jerusalem.

19. The Grotto of the Nativity, the place where Jesus is said to have been born, is an underground space which forms the crypt of the Church of the Nativity. It is situated underneath its main altar, and it is normally accessed by two staircases on either side of the chancel.

20. Logical conclusion: If there was no "Inn" and never had been, then why would they have used such an irrelevant term, as if to imply anything about an "Inn?" Therefore, it is most reasonable to accept the fact that an Inn had existed in the past and was still located in some semblance on that property in Bethlehem.

21. http://blog.adw.org/2014/07/what-were-typical-homes-like-in-jesus-time - "The kitchen as we know it did not exist. In small houses cooking was done out back on an open fire or in a fire pit. Utensils were kept in a chest. In larger houses the courtyard might be the place of the cooking fire and kitchen items were kept in a storeroom. Only the largest homes had a dedicated area with a fiery oven."

22. Star of Bethlehem – Wikipedia - "seventy days" This object was observed for over seventy days, possibly with no movement recorded. Ancient writers described comets as "hanging over" specific cities, just as the Star of Bethlehem was said to have "stood over" the "place" where Jesus was (the town of Bethlehem).

23. Matthew 2:7-12 NKJV

24. www.reference.com/world-view/jesus-given-gold-frankincense-myrrh-b3704f26ab6803ea - Why did the Magi bring gold, frankincense, and myrrh to Jesus? Other historians believe that gold, frankincense and myrrh have special symbolic meanings specifically for Jesus. They believe that gold represents Jesus's kingship, frankincense symbolizes his role as a priest in society and myrrh symbolizes the prefiguring of his death and embalming.

25. Matthew 2:13-14 NKJV

26. https://en.wikipedia.org/wiki/Sinai_Peninsula - The Sinai Peninsula has been a part of Egypt from the First Dynasty of ancient Egypt (c. 3100 BC). Note: It is unlikely that Joseph and Mary took Jesus on a journey of nearly 800 kilometers walk, but most likely stopped somewhere just over the line into Egypt, so they would be out of reach of Herod or his soldiers.

27. https://www.answers.com/Q/How_many_miles_did_Joseph_ and_Mary_travel_from_ Bethlehem_to_Egypt - How many miles did Joseph and Mary travel from Bethlehem to Egypt, and specifically to the part of Egypt that was an Egyptian-controlled territory? Herod's cruel actions fulfill a prophecy regarding the slaughter of innocent children. (Jeremiah 31:15) Their journey from Bethlehem to what was Egyptian-controlled territory (which was outside the jurisdiction of Herod) was at least 65 kilometers or 40 miles.

28. https://en.wikipedia.org/wiki/King%27s_Highway_ (ancient) ~ The King's Highway was a trade route of vital importance in the ancient Near East, connecting Africa with Mesopotamia. It ran from Egypt (Capital city of Heliopolis/Cairo) across the Sinai Peninsula to Aqaba, then turned northward across Transjordan, to Damascus and the Euphrates River. During the Roman period the road was called Via Regia. (This was during the time of the journey for Joseph, Mary and baby Jesus) Emperor Trajan rebuilt and renamed it Via Traiana Nova, under which name it served as a military and trade road.

29. https://amazingbibletimeline.com/blog/king-herod-the-great-new-facts ~ "The Gospels tell us that Christ's birth was shortly before Herod the Great died. Herod's death can be fixed with certainty. Josephus records an eclipse of the moon just before Herod passed on. This occurred on March 12th or 13th in 4 B.C. Josephus also tells us that Herod expired just before Passover. This feast took place on April 11th, in the same year, 4 B.C. From other details supplied by Josephus, we can pinpoint Herod the Great's demise as occurring between March 29th and April 4th in 4 B.C," generally considered the same year of Jesus' birth.

30. https://www.learnreligions.com/herod-the-great-enemy-of-jesus-christ-701064~ Herod the Great was a brutal man who killed his father-in-law, several of his ten wives, and two of his sons. He ignored the laws of God to suit himself and chose the favor of Rome over his own people. Herod's heavy taxes to pay for lavish projects forced an unfair burden on the Jewish citizens. This evil tyrant was an Idumean (a descendant of Esau) by ancestry.

31. Caution: Keep in mind that God had provisions for the family Joseph and Mary and the baby Jesus, so do not be tempted to over analyze the timelines of this beautiful story. Likely many things happened which are not given, but miracles of Divine provision must have taken place. It is my intention to keep the story to realistic and simplistic levels as much as possible. I do not just bend the narrative to accommodate orthodoxy or organized religion, and thus yield to the temptation to make it sound more sensational.

32. Luke 2:22 ~ gives the NT account of this story. / Leviticus 12 ~ Purification ceremony required for giving birth to a child, whether male or female.

33. Luke 2:29-35 CEV

34. Luke 2:38 NLT ~ Anna "came along just as Simeon was talking with Mary and Joseph, and she began praising God. She talked about the child to everyone who had been waiting expectantly for God to rescue Jerusalem."

35. Luke 2:39

36. Matthew 2:22-23

37. https://billygraham.org/answer/what-do-we-know-about-jesus-childhood

38. Mark 6:3 NLT

39. https://billygraham.org/answer/what-do-we-know-about-jesus-childhood

40. Matthew 13:54-56 ~ The names of his brothers are: James, Joseph, Simon, and Judas, and his sisters, whose names are not given. In Matthew 13:54-56 their names were given by the community leaders in the synagogue after Jesus returned to Nazareth immediately upon beginning his public ministry after age 30.

41. Luke 2:41-52 NKJV

Chapter 3
THE BACKSTORY BEGINS

Endnotes

1. Joshua 3-4

2. Joshua 2:24 CEV

3. Joshua 2:9-13 ERV -These were the words of Rahab to the two guests in her home.

4. www.yahoo.com ~ "Israelite" refers to: a member of the ancient Hebrew nation, especially in the period from the Exodus to the Babylonian Captivity (c. 12th to 6th centuries BC). / "Israeli" relates to the members of the modern country of Israel.

5. Genesis 38 ~ The entire chapter reveals the story of Judah and his character issues; introducing his indiscretion and ill treatment of his daughter in law, Tamar. It is his history, and it is what happened. We need not debate it but recognize that what Jeremiah said is so true. Jeremiah 17:9 says: "The heart is deceitful above all things, and desperately wicked; Who can know it?"

6. 1 Chronicles 2:1-11

7. Joshua 13-21 ~ The land was divided by God's commandment to result that 2.5 tribes were east of Jordan and the remaining 9.5 tribes were on the west side of Jordan. This was done by casting of lots.

8. Joshua 13-21~ After capturing the land of Canaan, Joshua and the Israelites divide up the land as an inheritance for the twelve tribes. The boundaries of land given to the tribe of Judah is seen in chapter 15. Salmon was a member of the tribe of Judah, so his land was within the land allocated to Judah and his portion was in Bethlehem.

9. Micah 5:2 CEV – "Bethlehem Ephratah, you are one of the smallest towns in the nation of Judah. But the LORD will choose one of your people to rule the nation— someone whose family goes back to ancient times."

10. Ruth 2:1 NLT – "Now there was a wealthy and influential man in Bethlehem named Boaz, who was a relative of Naomi's husband, Elimelech."

11. 1 Samuel 16:4

12. https://www.dictionary.com/browse/caravanserai – caravansary (kar-uh-van-suh-ree) In the Near East an inn, or something as versatile as a caravansary was usually designed with a large courtyard, for the overnight accommodation of caravans, which would accommodate travelers, animals, wagons, and whatever they carried with them.

13. https://en.wikipedia.org/wiki/Caravanserai – A caravanserai (or caravansary: / kærvænsra/) was a roadside inn where travelers (caravaners) could rest and recover from the day's journey. Caravanserais supported the flow of commerce, information and people across the network of trade routes covering Asia, North Africa and Southeast Europe, most notably the Silk Road. Although many were located along rural roads in the countryside, urban versions of caravanserais were also historically common in cities throughout the Islamic world, though they were often called by other names such as khan, wikala, or funduq.

14. https://www.biblestudytools.com/dictionary/bethlehem – "There is a church still existing, built by Constantine the Great (A.D. 330), called the "Church of the Nativity," over a grotto or cave called the 'holy crypt,' and said to be the 'stable' in which Jesus was born. This is perhaps the oldest existing Christian church in the world. Close to it is another grotto, where Jerome the Latin father is said to have spent thirty years of his life in translating the Scriptures into Latin."

15. Luke 2:1 NKJV – "And it came to pass in those days that a decree went out from Caesar Augustus that all the world should be registered."

16. Luke 2:7-16

17. Matthew 2:1-2 NKJV – "Now after Jesus was born in Bethlehem of Judea in the days of Herod the king, behold, wise men from the East came to Jerusalem, 2 saying, "Where is He who has been born King of the Jews? For we have seen His star in the East and have come to worship Him."

Chapter 4
DAVID AND A CIVIL WAR

Endnotes

1. The Golden Age of Israel ~ This is a term generally given to a period of approximately 120 years including the three 40-year reigns of Saul, David, and Solomon. Although these kings had very different leadership styles, under their leadership Israel transitioned from a primitive and disorganized state ruled by impulsive judges who thought only locally, to a national and centralized government.

2. en.wikipedia.org/wiki/David's Mighty Warriors ~ David's Mighty Warriors (also known as David's Mighty Men... "The Mighty Ones") were a group of 37 men in the Hebrew Bible who fought alongside King David and are identified in 2 Samuel 23:8–38... The International Standard Version calls them "David's special forces."

3. 2 Samuel 10 gives the full story of David's sins. 2 Samuel 12:1-23 NKJV gives the account of Nathan's visit to the palace on the morning of the birth of the child born from this affair.

4. 2 Samuel 12:7 KJV

5. https://www.dictionary.com/browse/larger-than-life ~ Larger-than-life definition, exceedingly imposing, impressive, or memorable, especially in appearance or forcefulness: a larger-than-life leader. /https://www.merriam-webster.com/dictionary/larger-than-life ~ of the sort legends are made of.

6. 2 Samuel 15:6

7. Proverbs 6:16-19 NLT

8. 2 Samuel 15:11 NKJV

9. https://hoshanarabbah.org/blog/2020/02/12/whats-so-significant-about-the-shofar-and-its-sound/ ~ "SHOFAR" ~ When Was the Shofar Sounded in Biblical Times? 1) The shofar was blown when a king was anointed (1 Kings 1:34, 39, 41; 2 Kings 9:13). 2) It signified the start or call to war (Joshua 6:4; Judges 3:27, 7:16, 20:3) It was sounded on the Day of Atonement to announce the jubilee year. (Leviticus 25:8–13) ~ FACT: Anytime the "trumpet" was blown in Israel, it was actually a shofar. Trumpet is the English word for shofar.

10. 2 Samuel 15:10 NKJV

11. 2 Samuel 15:13

12. https://www.dictionary.com/browse/coup-d-etat ~ coup d'état: a sudden decisive exercise of force in politics especially the violent overthrow or alteration of an existing government by a small group.

13. A Tale of Three Kings - A study in Brokenness, by Gene Edwards. Page 97-98 - ISBN 0-940232-03-0

14. Josephus, Book 7, Chapter 9:227

15. 2 Samuel 17:22 AMP

Chapter 5
BARZILLAI

Endnotes

1. https://www.dictionary.com/browse/caravanserai - caravansary (kar-uh-van-suh-ree) In the Near East an inn, or something as versatile as a caravansary was usually with a large courtyard, for the overnight accommodation of caravans, which would accommodate travelers, animals, wagons, and whatever they carried with them.

2. "Is there a Grandfather in the House?" ISBN: 978-0-9973515-0-7, by Ron A. Bishop. Chapter 28, "The Barzillai Story", Pages 241-254, (especially pages 241-246).

3. 1 Chronicles 3:1-2 NKJV - Absalom was David's third born son. "Now these were the sons of David who were born to him in Hebron: The firstborn was Amnon, by Ahinoam the Jezreelitess; the second, Daniel, by Abigail the Carmelitess; the third, Absalom the son of Maacah, the daughter of Talmai, king of Geshur; the fourth, Adonijah the son of Haggith."

4. Dictionary.com -Barzillai was a highlander: "highlands, a mountainous region or elevated part of a country." Sometimes a man from the mountains has the tone of more robust, or vigorous; certainly, a part of most countries where it is more remote, rural, or outside of the mainstream.

5. The name, Barzillai, means "Man of Iron", or "Iron-hearted". Without a doubt, we could consider this man to have been an Elder Statesman, as much as he was not celebrated beyond his local highlands. To recognize him for who he was, one had to travel across the Jordan and then to climb up into the highlands to find him. And then, it would not be so likely that everyone would be talking about him, as much as you would discover that for some reason there was a different nature about these hills.

6. www.behindthename.com/name/barzillai/submitted - "Derived from Aramaic or Hebrew barzillay meaning 'man of iron' or 'Iron-hearted', which was, in turn, derived from barzel 'iron'."

7. "Cattle post" ~ In the African nation of Botswana a cattle post is "where the animals are", or where livestock can roam freely. These are communal unfenced areas. Most of the residents of Setswana (moraka) claim their roots to be from those areas.

8. gnowfglins.com/author/erin ~ Although there are many versions known currently as The Balm of Gilead, made in remote places around the world, I have picked one, which gives this description: "This wonder salve soothes skin irritations such as eczema, cuts, rashes, burns, psoriasis, insect bites and stings, sunburn, athlete's foot, dry and scaly skin, chapped hands or cheeks, and prevents or heals diaper rash. Plus, it's like spring in a jar! [by Erin Vander Lugt]"

9. en.wikipedia.org/wiki/Balm_of_Gilead

10. https://www.healthline.com/health/eye-health/dominant-eye ~ In this story, is there a significance that should be considered regarding the right eye? ~ "Do we have a dominant eye? Just like we use one side of our body more than the other and have a dominant hand that we use for writing, most of us also have a dominant eye. A dominant eye isn't always about one having better vision, but rather one leading better than the other because of preference. Your dominant eye is the one that provides slightly more input to the visual cortex of your brain and relays information more accurately, such as the location of objects."

11. 1 Samuel 11 ~ Saul responded to the threat from Nahash and defended the city of Jabesh-Gilead.

12. 1 Samuel 31:2 and 1 Chronicles 10:2

13. 2 Samuel 4:4 NKJV ~ Jonathan, Saul's son, had a son who was lame in his feet. He was five years old when the news about Saul and Jonathan came from Jezreel; and his nurse took him up and fled. And it happened, as she made haste to flee, that he fell and became lame. His name was Mephibosheth.

14. 2 Samuel 17:27 MSG

15. 2 Samuel 18:17-33 ~ The runners were named Ahimaaz and the Cushite. The Cushite stated the story more clearly.

16. 2 Samuel 18:9-33 ~ Most translations simply state that Absalom's head was caught in the tree, but some state, his hair was caught in a tree. It seems logical either way.

17. 2 Samuel 19:14 ~ "Return, you and all your servants!"

18. Shimei mocked David as he was fleeing Jerusalem ~ 2 Samuel 16:5-13 Shimei fell and repented to David of his great indiscretion ~ 2 Samuel 19:18-23

19. Ziba gives an evil report (lies) to David about Mephibosheth ~ 2 Samuel 16:1-4 Mephibosheth tells David (the Truth) about what happened ~ 2 Samuel 19:24-30

20. 2 Samuel 19:18 NKJV ~ "Then a ferryboat went across to carry over the king's household, and to do what he thought good."

21. Josephus Book 7, Chapter 11:2:264

22. 2 Samuel 19:34-37 CEB

23. 2 Samuel 19:37 NKJV

24. Josephus Book 7, Chapter 11:4:274

25. 2 Samuel 19:38 AMP ~ David had invited Barzillai to accompany him. However, in reviewing the response to consider Chimham, it was much better, as the king could see that the older man was not strong. In David's mind, it appears that a lasting heritage could better be served by going with Chimham. Although little is said, David was pleased at the wisdom of his friend in bringing Chimham into the conversation.

Chapter 6
David Searches His Soul

Endnotes

1. https://www.bible-history.com/sketches/ancient/tomb-absalom.html ~ "Tomb of Absalom" – Located on the Eastern slope of the Kidron Valley, on the east side of Jerusalem.

2. 2 Samuel 20

3. Josephus Book 7, Chapter 11:4:274 ~ David made a promise to Barzillai that he would be good to Chimham and generous to him. These are the recorded words as told by Josephus: "I dismiss thee, but thou shalt grant me thy son Chimham, and upon him I will bestow all sorts of good things."

4. The two spies whom Joshua had sent to "spy out the land of Canaan, were technically unnamed and yet we do know that Salmon, by some means had met Rahab and chosen her as his wife in that same time period. As a result of the resulting conjecture by many scholars we have come to see Salmon as one of those spies. He was clearly impressed with how she had expressed her own grasp of the place of Israel with God in the bigger picture of things. Joshua 6:23

5. Matthew 1:5 MSG ~ "Abraham had Isaac, Isaac had Jacob, Jacob had Judah and his brothers, Judah had Perez and Zerah (the mother was Tamar), Perez had Hezron, Hezron had Aram, Aram had Amminadab, Amminadab had Nahshon, Nahshon had Salmon, Salmon had Boaz (his mother was Rahab), Boaz had Obed (Ruth was the mother), Obed had Jesse, Jesse had David, and David became king." Matthew 1:5 ERV ~ ERV ~ "Salmon

was the father of Boaz. (His mother was Rahab.) Boaz was the father of Obed. (His mother was Ruth.) Obed was the father of Jesse."

6. https://www.christianity.com/bible/commentary.php?com=spur&b=19&c=105 ~ Charles Spurgeon wrote these words in his volume called: The Treasury of David wrote regarding Psalm 105, especially verse 8: "This historical psalm was evidently composed by King David, for the first fifteen verses of it were used as a hymn at the carrying up of the ark from the house of Obededom, and we read in 1Ch 16:7, "Then on that day David delivered first this psalm to thank the Lord, into the hand of Asaph and his brethren." Such a song was suitable for the occasion, for it describes the movements of the Lord's people and his guardian care over them in every place, and all this on account of the covenant of which the ark, then removing, was a symbol."

7. Smith's Bible Dictionary ~ Chimham ~ (2 Samuel 19:37-40) David appears to have bestowed on him a possession at Bethlehem, on which, in later times, an inn or khan was standing. (Jeremiah 41:17)

8. Josephus Book 7, Chapter 15:1:387, Josephus, Book 7, Chapter 9:227

9. https://www.dictionary.com/browse/caravanserai ~ pronounced: [kar-uh-van-suh-ree] ~ (in the Near East) an inn, usually with a large courtyard, for the overnight accommodation of caravans.

10. https://www.merriam-webster.com/dictionary/caravan ~ caravan ~ a company of travelers on a journey through desert or hostile regions.

11. https://en.wikipedia.org/wiki/Caravanserai ~ Caravanserai ~ a roadside inn where travelers (caravaners) could rest and recover from the day's journey. Caravanserais supported the flow of commerce, information and people across the network of trade routes covering Asia, North Africa and Southeast Europe, most notably the Silk Road.

12. Luke 2:7 KJV The reason for the comment: "because there was no room for them in the inn," Is because there was historical proof that there was a traditional Inn in Bethlehem. This inn had been there back to the days of Jeremiah 41:7 and all the way back to the days of King David. This was actually on the site of where David grew up with his family. It was his inheritance which he had passed to Chimham as a gift. There was a physical grotto behind it where the sheep were kept.

13. Matthew 1:17 KJV

14. https://www.gotquestions.org/Davidic-covenant.html ~ References to confirm that the Messiah will come from the lineage of David: 2 Samuel 7, Matthew 21:9, Jeremiah 23:5; Isaiah 9:7; 11:1; Luke 1:32, 69; Acts 13:34 and Revelation 3:7

15. Mark 10:46-48 ERV

Chapter 7
A PROPHETIC CONNECTION

Endnotes

1. 2 Kings 25

2. Jeremiah 27:6 NKJV

3. IBID

4. scribblenauts.fandom.com/wiki/Quicksand ~ Quicksand is a loose wet sand that yields easily to pressure and sucks in anything resting on or falling into it.

5. Ebed-Melech, The Ethiopian Court Official ~ There is reason to believe that there is a connection in the history of the Queen of Sheba from the days of Solomon (I Kings 10) and the treasurer who was on assignment from Candace, queen of the Ethiopians (Acts 8:27), and the Coptic Churches, one of the oldest branches of Christianity, from Egypt. To do your own study consider starting with these scriptures to do your own research: I Kings 10:1, Isaiah 56:3-8, Jeremiah 38:5-13, Acts 8:27.

6. Jeremiah 38:5-13

7. Jeremiah 39:15-18 NKJV

8. Jeremiah 39:14, and 40:6

9. 2 Kings 25:24 MSG

10. Josephus Book 10, 9:1 ~ An account of how Nebuzaradan released Jeremiah from Zedekiah's prison.

11. Jeremiah 40:13-16 Gedaliah essentially said, "You don't know Ishmael like I know him. You are wrong and must not do what you have said."

12. Josephus Book 10, 9:4 ~ An account of the treachery of Ishmael against Gedaliah.

13. https://www.chabad.org/library/article_cdThis o/aid/4825/jewish/Gedaliah.htm

14. Jeremiah 41:15

15. Jeremiah 41:17

16. https://www.dictionary.com/browse/caravanserai ~ caravansary (kar-uh-van-suh-ree) In the Near East an inn, or something as versatile as a caravansary was usually designed with a large courtyard, for the overnight accommodation of caravans, which would accommodate travelers, animals, wagons, and whatever they carried with them.

17. www.thenamemeaning.com/bethlehem ~ The meaning of the name, Bethlehem, is "House of Bread."

18. Jeremiah 41:17

19. Jeremiah 41:16-17 AMP

Epilogue

Endnotes

1. Psalm 14:1 CEV

2. Mark 10:46-52

3. Jeremiah 17:9 NKJV

4. John 3:3

5. https://factsandtrends.net/2018/02/21/billy-grahams-life-ministry-by-the-numbers

6. https://www.youtube.com/watch?v=g3krcCSrJjo ~ A video of one of Billy Graham's calls to repentance.

More From Ron A. Bishop

THE JOSEPH STORY
Treachery, Betrayal, and Redemption

THE MENTOR KING
**Heart Revealing Days
in the Life of King David**

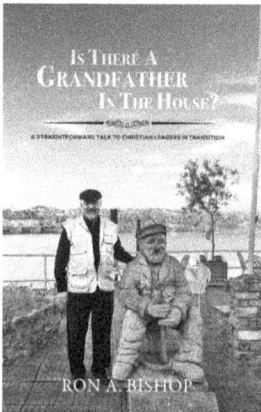

IS THERE A GRANDFATHER IN THE HOUSE?
**A Straightforward Talk to
Christian Leaders in Transition**

To Contact the Author:

WWW.SHEPHERDSHAPERS.COM

www.ingramcontent.com/pod-product-compliance
Lightning Source LLC
LaVergne TN
LVHW041200080426
835511LV00006B/683